WORK

IS NOT A PLACE

NOT

Our Lives and Our Organizations in the Post-Jobs Economy

LINDA NAZARETH

First edition November 2018

Book and Cover Design by Jana Rade, impact studios

ISBN: 978-0-9936510-2-1 (Book)
ISBN: 978-0-9936510-3-8 (Ebook)

Published by Relentless Press
www.relentlesseconomics.com

If you are interested in having Linda Nazareth be a keynote speaker at your event, please contact speaking@relentlesseconomics.com

For Maddie.

CONTENTS

EVERYTHING IS ON THE TABLE

Sometimes it all comes together. Sometimes it makes perfect sense for workers to be employed and for companies to employ them. Sometimes a company manages to inspire people, and they give their best back, and in return, the product ends up being more than the sum of the parts. These were some of my thoughts as I took the stage as the host of an employee-engagement event put on by a major financial institution.

The venue, a trendy gallery space in a gentrifying part of Toronto, was lovely. Rain pelted outside, but none of the busload of specially chosen employees seemed to care. The chair of the organization was retiring within months, a successor had been chosen, and this event was an opportunity to say goodbye and hello and to hear both men's thoughts on the company's future. More important, it was a chance for the employees to share their views—starting with the discussion in the room, but continuing as the dialogue moved online and others chimed in.

More often than not, I am a keynote speaker, so the opportunity to host was an interesting one for me. I had been asked to do so because of my insights into economics and the future of work (as opposed to my television work, which often leads to gigs of this sort). But this was not an occasion for me to share my views: rather, I was there to draw on what I knew in order to keep the conversation going, to ask pertinent questions and encourage people to give their opinions. I was perfectly honest when I opened by telling the audience that it was a privilege to be in the room with them. They were on the front lines of the ways in which trends and technology are reshaping the economy, and I appreciated the chance to hear about their experiences.

What struck me about this particular group was quite simply how happy they seemed. Happy, enthusiastic, engaged, committed—those were the words I would use to describe their mood that Friday afternoon. Of course, this was a preselected group, and there was a certain excitement in being out of the office and in a glamorous space alongside the company's elite. It was more than that, though. I have worked in places where the experience would have been radically different; if management needed to fill a room with happy workers, their best bet would have been to hire actors to impersonate them. This group was different, and the discussion reflected it. They shared stories; they asked about company direction; they laughed a great deal. They were upbeat and they acted like a team, and those are not easy things to fake. I could feel that they had made a commitment to the company and the company had done the same to them, and that those commitments were paying dividends. As company structures go, it was pretty traditional—the same model, essentially, as had existed for decades. For these folk, it was working.

But for how long? It's possible that everyone in that room, from the highest level of C-Suite executives down to the newest interns, would be better off not getting too comfortable with that model—or any other, for that matter. The reality is that what works right now may not be what works tomorrow, or next year, or 10 years after that. Our current corporate and workforce model is changing quickly, and it is in the best interests of everyone involved to be prepared.

Companies, firms, corporations—a couple of centuries ago, almost no one worked at any of the above. These days, having a job and getting paid, maybe with some benefits, seems like a pretty fundamental thing, but it was not always thus. To be sure, people have always worked, but the model of the modern workplace—where a large company employs lots of workers—is a fairly recent phenomenon. It has been the norm for a couple of hundred years at most, an ideal prompted by some dramatic economic history. Now, more economic history is being made around us, and with it will come a new norm in terms of how we work.

SCARIER THAN FICTION

Let's not sugarcoat it: things are changing, and change is scary. Every day, we are bombarded with alarmist headlines: "Really Smart Think Tank Has Determined that a Robot Can Do Your Job Really Soon and Way Better"; "Six Guys in Silicon Valley Are Becoming Mega-Billionaires and Everyone Else Is Getting Poorer"; "In the Future, Your Kids Will Not Be Able to Find Employment and Will Live with You Forever." The concept of going to work is changing; the concept of having a job is changing; the concept of picking a career and working at it for the bulk of a lifetime is changing too. It's unsettling, to say the least. Looking at the next 10, 20, or 50 years, it's fair to say that everything is on the table in terms of what we have come to associate with the norms of "work."

It's also hard to discern truth from fiction, to sort out the different narratives regarding how the labor market is evolving. The robots-are-coming stories are catchy, to be sure, and they crop up with alarming regularity, but the not-enough-workers stories can give them a run for their money. We hear of brutal talent wars in Silicon Valley that lead to software engineers being paid like rock stars. We hear of convicts being released from prisons in Idaho to do farm work that no one else can or wants to do. In both the United States and Canada, the unemployment rate is hovering at levels not seen since the 1960s, thanks to strong economies and a demographically induced shortage of workers. Thirty or 40 years ago, it seems, people forgot to have kids, and now we can't fill positions. We need to sort out which narrative is going to rule, and whether different ones will be dominant for different groups of people.

Why do we need to do this? Because the future of work matters a lot, and not just to workers. In a way, the "labor market"—or "work," when you get right down to it—is a synonym for "the economy." Up until now, the two have basically functioned simultaneously. That might be changing a bit (we'll explore that later), but it's a truism we've come to accept. Like it or not, we have created a work-to-live economy, where the majority of households rely, to a greater or lesser degree, on what they earn in the market economy to power their consumption. You work, you earn money, and you use that money to pay for food and housing and whatever else you want to buy. You might skip that process if you have a trust fund from Grandpa or are unable to work, but those are the exceptions rather than the rule. And if we are going to change the rules on what work is, we have to realize that we're changing many other things along with it.

Work matters for other reasons as well. For some of us, what we "do" is at the center of our identity, of who we are. There may be a generational component to that, and perhaps a gender bias too. Ironically, this is true despite the fact that a lot of people claim to hate their job. According to a 2017 Gallup survey, only 30 percent of U.S. employees (and only 15 percent of those in the world) are "engaged" at work (basically defined as enthusiastic about and committed to their jobs).[1] But engaged or not, work is what we expect of ourselves, and of each other. In North America in particular, there is a deep distrust of not working. Outside of youth and the retired, the only groups that seem to legitimately be allowed out of the labor force are full-time students and stay-at-home parents (and the latter is, in fact, a source of great controversy, as evidenced by the "Mommy Wars" between working and stay-at-home mothers that has been highlighted in the media in recent years).

For so many of us, work is not just about earning money. For better or worse, working and the work we do help us to create an identity, as well as to make social connections. At a time when "loneliness" is apparently becoming a societal scourge—one that some say has the same health outcome as smoking 15 cigarettes a day[2]—that is no small consideration. And so we have looked to work and to workplaces to fill a lot of different needs. What exactly are we planning to replace them with if they disappear?

* * *

As an economist, I have spent my entire career fascinated by the way that demographic and labor market trends affect everything else. As a speaker who has addressed conferences and companies, it's a topic I like to cover, and one that is always of interest. Whether I'm speaking to investors, companies, industry organizations, or other groups, the future of work is always pertinent.

I have been through a few career transitions myself. Although I've always been an economist, I have had some pretty varied experiences. I've worked for government and a large financial firm, and (most unusually for someone in my profession) I spent a decade as an on-air personality for the Business News Network (Canada's equivalent to CNBC). I have also worked as a consultant, taught in an MBA program, written three previous books, been a columnist in print and online, been a keynote speaker, and served as a senior fellow at a think tank. (With the exception of teaching, I still do most of those things.) I even got a taste of politics by running for my local town council; I didn't win, but it was a good experience just the same.

In the span of my own career, technology has changed things dramatically. When I started work in the early 1990s, some my co-workers were aghast that they might have to learn to *type*. At the time, the secretarial ranks were dwindling, and men and women in management positions were being encouraged to draft their own documents on personal computers. (I think some of the real stalwarts managed to limp toward retirement without ever sinking to that oh-so-demeaning level.) A few decades later, I do a lot of my own work wherever I want, whether that is at home, in a coffee shop, or waiting for my daughter at a skating rink. Somewhere along the line, computers became laptops, and the internet put the world at my fingertips. My working hours are not nine-to-five anymore (for good and bad), and I do not have to go to a designated place of work to get access to office equipment. Now, my "office" is where my computer and I happen to be, and my "hours" are whatever happens to make sense on a given day. There's no question that I've experienced significant change in my career—as I'm sure many of you have as well—but the changes coming down the pike are going to be even more dramatic. People already sense this, and as a result, many are afraid for themselves or their children—much more so than those folk who were told to learn keyboarding ever were. That's why I decided to write this book: to sort through the tangle of misinformation and fear and take a good, hard look at where work is going—and where it will take everything and everyone else as it goes.

ARE COMPANIES DONE?

Given the central place that work holds in our lives, it's interesting to see how our ideas about work are changing. For example, it's getting harder to pin down exactly what "work" is. The phrase "I'm going to work" may still apply to a large swath of people, but the notion of that workplace, or even of "work" itself, does not evoke the rock-solid permanency that it used to. The tenure of a job has decreased—people change jobs frequently, and many are forced to retire years before they would like to—and a workplace is no longer necessarily an office. A core group of people may still have one job and one workplace, but that core is dwindling. Everyone else is living a new reality and figuring it out as they go along. For some, the local coffee shop has become a creative and acceptable alternative (just pop by your local favorite some morning if you doubt this). Other solutions and accommodations are taking shape as well, and some are much more dramatic than setting up a laptop at a Starbucks.

* * *

We have been through revolutions in how we work and how we get compensated before. The idea of work being a place—"I'm going to work"—is a fairly new one. Firms as we know them only started taking shape a couple of hundred years ago, and when they did, they were a revolutionary idea in a revolutionary time. But perhaps we are at another revolutionary point in history. For the past century or two, we have grown accustomed to a model in which most of us work for, and are paid by, a single employer. Next up, apparently, is an age in which many of us work for ourselves and are paid by many employers. Call it a cottage industry for the 21st century.

Thanks to technology, the transaction costs of getting work done (that is, what you have to spend to get workers to do needed work as necessary) have dropped precipitously in many industries. When speaking to audiences, I often illustrate this by using my experience as an author. When I wrote my first two books, in 2001 and 2007, the cover illustrations were done by graphic designers who were employed by the companies publishing my work. I am not sure how much it actually "cost" to design those covers, but the individuals involved would have been paid employee benefits as well as salaries. For my third book, in 2013, I decided to give self-publishing a whirl. The cover was put together by a freelancer recommended by the company that helped with typesetting the book. The cost was around $600, and it took a few weeks to complete.

By the time I wrote *this* book, I was more familiar with the self-publishing process. I knew, for example, that it was a good idea to get a book promo page on my website so that people could learn about the book even before I wrote it. I needed a cover image for that, and I wanted to get one up in a hurry. I turned to a site called Fiverr, which matches freelancers from around the world with those seeking to use their services. Originally, people offered work for five dollars (a "fiver"); prices have gone up a bit over time. I'd used the site for a few other things, including business card design, and was happy with the quality of the work I'd gotten.

So, I typed "book cover design" into the search field and started scrolling through the pages of individuals that came up—some from the United States and Canada, but many from as far away as Ecuador, Sweden, Pakistan, and Macedonia. I picked a designer whose work I liked (from Nigeria), contacted him, and told him what I wanted. Within three days—which included time to go back and forth on revisions—I had a cover for my website. The cost? Forty dollars—plus the $10 tip (25 percent) I also provided. Audiences always gasp when I tell them this. Some like the cover and others don't, but the quality is absolutely on par with anything you'd see in a bookstore. Thanks to the existence of the internet and the site, I was able to pay less for the job and get it done more efficiently. That made me happy. The Nigerian designer was apparently happy as well, as was Fiverr, which processes thousands of such transactions a day. The cost of those transactions to the buyer is far below what it was in the days before the internet made portfolios full of work from all over the globe available to every would-be author sitting in Toronto and looking for a book cover design. The work is still getting done and workers are still getting paid. They are just working under a different model, and they are selling their work rather than blocks of their time. And, even if you argue that graphic designers always tended to work as freelancers, the fact is that technology allows for the final buyer of their work to deal directly with the artist, no agency or agent necessary.

Not every job can get done by typing a few keystrokes into a website, but these days, quite a few can. If I, as a writer and independent worker, can pick and choose the skills I want to buy, then there is no reason why larger companies cannot as well. Of course, they are doing so already, and as they do, they are considering new models of work. The Fiverr approach is one way to get things done. Another is the "Hollywood Model," in which people are assembled to work on a particular project and are dispersed when it's finished. Each of those models fits within the so-called Gig Economy, wherein people get paid for the gigs they do by the people who need their services for a specific project, rather than by an employer who hires them for a long period of time.

Companies that hire workers may never vanish altogether, but when there are so many ways to get work done, it's natural that they are going to explore different models. The flip side is that workers can look for different models of how to work. It's a Pandora's box, without a doubt, but we've opened it now and there is no going back.

REIMAGINING EVERYTHING

And so we have the reality: costs must be kept down, and workers must be the best they can possibly be. In the story of labor demand, there is nothing so new about that. What *is* new, however, is that we are at an inflection point—this time in which we find ourselves, when two major trends are taking shape on the labor-supply side. One says that we are headed into a demographic crisis and that we will not have enough workers to do whatever amount of work exists. The other says technology is changing so fast that there isn't going to be enough work to go around. If we accept that strands of both narratives are going to hold true, one way or another, we must concede that we've got a wild ride ahead.

It is so easy to judge the changes happening in the labor market and to categorize them as "bad" or "good." Our economy has been built around the concept of the full-time job. It shapes our weeks and weekends, determines when we take holidays, and is the major determinant of what we can consume. Banks will rarely loan money for a car or a mortgage unless someone has either significant accumulated assets (rare, if they are asking for the loan) or a full-time job (the norm). Of course, it seems wrong to question that model.

Still, it would be a mistake to say that the movement toward a new model of work is all bad. After all, not everyone *wants* to be an employee. Remember that Gallup poll that looked at how many workers were actually "engaged"? It told us that 32 percent of U.S. workers put themselves in that category in 2015, with 50.8 percent saying they were not engaged and another 17.2 percent saying they were actively disengaged.

Not that involuntary unemployment usually improves people's moods, but perhaps there is a happy medium between full-time employment and being permanently out of a job. With the rise of contract work, gig work, side hustles, remote work, and part-time jobs, it's clear that not everyone who doesn't "go to work" at a designated place is unhappy. Many, given a nice boost by the technology that allows them to work this way, are doing it by choice and would be hard-pressed to choose traditional employment. Indeed, with the move to more flexible schedules, many workers are likely happier with their work lives, if not their incomes.

And so we have choices on the table. Choices for employers, certainly, but choices for would-be employees as well. As much as companies can choose to pare down their staffs, employees can choose whether they want to be part of the corporate team, or part of their own. Choosing the latter may necessitate making a different series of choices about how they live and spend their money, and those choices, in turn, may affect the broader economy. If corporations are no longer acting as an anchor, everything else may become a little less rigid. And we have societal choices ahead as well. Do we want to legislate the way that companies can operate and pay people? Or do we want to change the rules to encourage people to set up their own safety nets and savings plans? Or maybe that's a role for government. Some think the world ahead will necessitate that we raise everyone's taxes and pay out a universal basic income. What will it mean if we do that—or if we don't?

Will jobs exist in the future? Of course they will, and firms too. The reality, though, is that we are looking at a much messier, more complicated future than we have ever seen before, at least as it relates to the labor market. Figuring out how to work through that mess will be a challenge, but doing so starts with understanding what is happening now, and what will happen next. That is what this book provides: a look backward, to the history that brought up here, and forward, at the trends that will take us into the future. It also means recognizing that, in a sense, this is nothing new: the labor market has gone through many transitions already, starting back when jobs didn't exist as we know them today, and firms didn't either. More recently, we've seen other kinds of transitions, including the entry of women into the workforce, and several occupational and industrial shifts. Notably, starting in the 1970s, we saw a shift from job security to much more insecurity than we had ever seen before. Now we're in the midst of another transition—to a time when it makes more sense for companies to have fewer employees than ever before, and where, in fact, it may make more sense for companies to not even exist. *Agility* is the buzzword for the future, and it will describe both employees and companies. Are you ready?

PART 1

CHAPTER 1

IT'S A LIVING: PAST, PRESENT, AND FUTURE

The ad ran in 2015, on an online site that specializes in securing household staff for the aristocracy. Reading it, you get the impression that these particular aristocrats want an awful lot for their money:

"Housekeeper sought for a large family home in Norfolk. . . . Main duties will include: cleaning all areas of the house to a high standard; caring for and maintaining the home owners' clothing; cleaning silverware and glassware; purchasing groceries and general provisions for the house; and dealing with deliveries. On occasions, the role will also involve the preparation of meals, assisting with childcare and caring for dogs."

Strivers, you might say? Barely-there rich, barely-there nobility who have no idea who does what on a household staff and how many people it takes to run a "large family home"? Well, no, not really. The ad was placed by the Duke and Duchess of Cambridge (you might know them as Will and Kate), who at the time were parents to one small child. The duke, grandson of the Queen and second in line to the throne, would surely know that you need separate people to polish silver and take care of children. After all, he and the duchess have both said they watch *Downton Abbey*.

Downton Abbey, for anyone who hasn't seen it, is a historical television drama created by Julian Fellowes, first broadcast in the United Kingdom and then imported to North America (the last season wrapped in 2015). *Downton* tells the story of the Earl of Grantham and his family, who live in a grand estate (in Yorkshire, not Norfolk), and the downstairs staff that serves them over a period that starts before the First World War and ends in the late 1920s. The show is a neat piece of economic history, illustrating the demand for and supply of what were then called "servants," and the way those things changed over time.

Anyone who has gotten their economic history from *Downton* would be puzzled by the lack of specialization sought by these modern-day royals. Being a "housekeeper," ordering groceries, doing housework, and prepping some meals is one thing. Adding clothes maintenance (which I'm guessing doesn't just mean throwing in a few loads of laundry now and again), along with keeping the silverware gleaming, the kids happy, and the dogs fed is quite another. On *Downton*, a butler attends to the big picture. He supervises the footmen, who clean silver; a cook, assisted by kitchen maids, who orders groceries and does food prep; a lady's maid, who attends to the countess's clothing; and a butler, who attends to the earl's. There are also lots of housemaids to do the cleaning and the scut work. Even assuming that this duke and duchess have a handful of other staff, and that their "large family home" is somewhat smaller than an estate, a single "housekeeper" still seems like a huge downgrade.

This huge downgrade for those hiring domestic labor mirrors an upgrade for workers. In the *Downton* years, individuals who would have been lucky to get work as farmhands (or to marry a farmhand) were thrilled to get work "in service" on large estates.

As the decades passed, however, economic conditions shifted. Industrialization spread throughout the developed world, and with it, the demand for labor increased. Although domestic labor never exactly disappeared, its ranks were certainly depleted as other opportunities presented themselves for those who would previously have looked for work on the nearest estate. These days, it is no longer cheap to acquire a domestic staff, which means that the average aristocrat (or even the average royal) will have to come to terms with getting fewer staff for their money than they did a hundred years ago.

Only about a century has passed between the *Downton* era—when large estates were full of under-butlers and such—and now, when the second in line to the throne hires a jack-of-all-trades to service his estate. Many things have changed in the broader world over that time period, and many things are changing now. Although we are not likely headed back to a time when labor is so plentiful and cheap that silver polishers will flourish, we are rethinking the industrial model that has become the norm. We should not be too quick to say that that will be to the detriment of workers: on the contrary, some trends are in their favor. What we should do, though, is remind ourselves that when it comes to the labor market, change has been the norm—and it will continue to be so as we move forward.

A BRIEF HISTORY OF WORK

These days, assuming you are in good health, you likely work for a living or are expected to (unless you are relatively young, relatively old, a student, taking care of family at home, or born with a trust fund). Working for pay is how we gather the resources to afford food, lodging, and everything else we want and need. But this was not always the case.

Once upon a time, "working" meant working to live. The earliest societies fell under the "hunter-gatherer" umbrella; people basically spent their time looking for food to eat. At some point, those societies transformed into an "agrarian" model, where food was grown and people worked as agricultural laborers, a transition called the Neolithic Revolution. In fact, there were a series of Neolithic Revolutions that started around 10,000 to 8,000 BCE and spread around the world.

By the time the ancient Egyptians started developing irrigation projects around 3100 BCE, they had devised systems that allowed them to organize and make use of vast quantities of labor. Over time, civilizations developed, and new labor specializations did as well. Artisans became skilled at pottery and metalwork, and there were early versions of physicians.

Still, for a very long time, agriculture—or working on family farms—was how most workers spent their time. In Celtic Britain (from about 650 BCE onward), for example, the majority of people were farmers, but the skilled trades had started to take shape as well. There were carpenters, potters, leatherworkers, bronzesmiths, and jewelers. Still, it would be many years before societies became anything other than primarily agrarian. By the Middle Ages, most people worked, including women and children, but they did so mainly on farms or in their own homes.

In those days, you could say there was something of a gig economy in place. That is, any kind of manufacturing or food production was generally done inside of people's homes, and there wasn't one employer who took on workers of any kind on a contract basis. Textile making in Britain, for example, was done in the homes of spinners and weavers.[3] Artisans worked for many clients, and their work defined them so absolutely that they became named for what they did—Bakers or Millers or Smiths.

The first known factory was arguably developed in 1768 in Cromford, England, when a man named Richard Arkwright invented a spinning frame that could produce multiple threads at once. It was a revolutionary invention—a textile machine that could produce fabric on a scale not seen previously. Hiring a few workers and having them work out of their own homes was no longer a viable scenario—the machines needed to be housed in a central location—so, all of a sudden, there was a need for factories to house both the machinery and the increasing numbers of people who could operate it. And so Arkwright built his first textile mill in 1774. There were not enough people in Cromford to handle the work, so he brought in more from the surrounding areas. Although some of Arkwright's practices are no longer common today (he paid his workers with special currency that could only be used at his own establishments), the Mill at Cromford changed the game, and the workforce as we know it started to take shape.[4]

THE ERA OF THE FIRM

By about 1776 (the year economist Adam Smith penned *The Wealth of Nations*, a treatise on free markets), the Industrial Revolution was taking shape. Britain, its birthplace, had natural resources (such as coal) as well as imports (such as cotton produced in its colonies) that could be worked into finished products; new machines had been invented and new production processes were in hand. As a result, an era of industrialization began in earnest in Britain. Factories began to spring up, and people migrated in large numbers from rural areas to cities to work in them.

At least in its early stages, this manifestation of the labor market did not lead to a better life for the majority of workers. In the textile industry, for example, child labor was the norm, with many children working 12 hours a day under terrible conditions. The situation was even worse in the coal industry, where young children sometimes worked underground. Over time, however, workers began to share in some of the spoils of what were rapidly growing economies in the industrialized countries, and their standard of living did rise as a result. According to researchers Nicholas Crafts and Terence Mills, between 1840 and 1910 "real wages" (wages that have been adjusted for the effects of inflation) more than doubled. The story is straightforward: technological innovation led to productivity gains, which eventually led to wage gains.[5]

It was, for all intents and purposes, the Golden Age of the Firm, and it continued well into the 20th century. Writing in 1937, economist Ronald Coase (who eventually won a Nobel Prize for his work) published a paper called "The Nature of the Firm," the central tenet of which was that firms exist because they offer a cheaper form of operation than going to the market continuously for resources. Economic theory would tell us that it makes sense to negotiate for the best prices on things as you need them. If you need a worker to do a task, for example, the "invisible hand" of economics suggests that the ideal would be to put the task up for bid and then get the lowest price for the work. But doing that again and again when you need work done continuously doesn't make sense; in fact, it means incurring hefty transaction costs each time you need to find workers. As such, it is often simpler for firms to hire workers and agree to pay them a salary as long as they show up, ready and able to work. Firms exist, Coase concluded, because transaction costs exist—and transaction costs muddy the purchase of resources.

As the industrialized economy grew, firms prospered and workers continued to share in the spoils. Eventually, workers at some firms even began receiving "benefits," as companies tried to determine how best to attract and keep employees. In 1875, the American Express railroad company was the first to introduce a retirement pension; soon, large manufacturing and utility companies followed suit. The practice reached its peak in 1970, when about 45 percent of private-sector workers were covered.[6] In retrospect, that might have been the golden age for workers, or at least *a* golden age, in a no-brainer kind of way. The prevalent model of work was that of full-time employment, with a long tenure, if that was what the employee wished, and it came with benefits as well. It worked well enough for everyone, at least for a time.

A few years into the 1970s, however, the industrial model started to transform. A spike in oil prices and a rise in a new phenomenon called "inflation" had companies questioning their business plans. Unemployment rates in industrial countries rose as companies resorted to layoffs in the wake of economic uncertainty. A bond of sorts between workers and employers was broken as the notion of employment for life became less prevalent.

Things did not improve in the 1980s and '90s, as a series of vicious recessions continued to force tough economic decisions. The unemployment rate went up and down, eventually hitting historically low levels in the United States and Canada by the end of the 1990s. Other indicators, however, suggested that things were not quite so rosy. One barometer of economic health is the "labor-force participation rate," or the proportion of people who *choose* to seek work—meaning that at any given time they are either employed or unemployed, as opposed to in school, home with their families, or in early retirement. Often, economists choose to look at the participation rate of "prime age" males (those between the ages of 25 and 54), since that group tends to be the most stable in terms of consistently seeking work. That participation rate started to decline in the mid-1990s, in concert with the fall of the manufacturing industry and the rise of technology, which suggests that something was going amiss for this group of workers.

In fact, by 2005—a good three years before the global economic crisis took place—companies were already shifting away from the model of full-time, permanent employment that had been the norm for so long. According to economists Lawrence Katz of Harvard and Alan Krueger of Princeton, the proportion of workers in the U.S. who were in what they defined as "alternative work arrangements" rose from 10.7 percent in 2005 to 15.8 percent in 2015. Put another way, virtually all of the job growth seen in the United States over that period was in the alternative work category, which they defined as including such things as those who work for temporary help agencies, on-call workers, independent contractors, and workers provided by contract firms (say, a janitor who is employed by an outside company rather than the company whose premises he cleans). That last category, in fact, was the fastest growing over the time period.

Amidst a global recession and a focus on that old chestnut of economic indicators, the "unemployment rate," the shift that was happening in the labor force was almost overlooked. It was an important one, however: something had changed in the old relationship between firms and employees, and there was no going back.

WHY WORKERS ARE GOING OUT OF FASHION

As we head for the third decade of the 21st century, we are reaching a point where companies can pick and choose just how much of their work they want to have done by actual employees, and how much they want to get done by other means—whether those means be nontraditional workers or robots or other forms of technology. If a company sticks with human workers, it can choose for those workers to be full-time, part-time, contract, on-site, or remote—or any combination thereof. More and more, it makes sense for companies to eschew a one-size-fits-all model in terms of hiring. The reasons are manifold.

To start, there is the fact that Ronald Coase—the economist who figured out that it made sense to form firms—was on the mark, but he was writing in a different era. Those transaction costs that Coase wrote about have plummeted for many companies. Just as Uber makes it easy to push a button and have a ride show up, other forms of technology have, in a sense, Uber-ized employees. Temporary help agencies have been around for decades, but in recent years they have changed form. Once used to plug in a clerk or a receptionist, these days they are increasingly an option to find an engineer or a chief financial officer. Or why use an agency at all? Online platforms such as Upwork list hundreds of workers in all fields. If she needs to, a human resources manager at a firm in, say, Detroit, can find someone close to home and have them come into the office. If the work can be done virtually, the world is her oyster. Of course, some work needs to be done quickly and on-site, and there are platforms for that as well. TaskRabbit,[7] for example, lets you find someone in your neighborhood who is willing to help move boxes or put together that Stuva loft bed from Ikea that looked much more straightforward in the store (no wonder Ikea recently bought TaskRabbit). For a long time, it made perfect economic sense to create big companies, employ many workers, and uphold a traditional model of compensation; it makes less sense going forward.

Quite apart from the fact that it is now easy to pull labor together at short notice, a confluence of factors is discouraging companies from routinely hiring large staffs and keeping them on for long periods of time. That is not to say that there is not, and will not be, demand for certain workers. A huge demand for "superstars," for example, will allow them to remain in a strong bargaining position. For another segment of workers, however, there will be a "hollowing out" that will leave many with precarious job prospects. In between will be a core of workers who may or may not gain traditional employment, or more likely will find themselves moving between traditional and nontraditional work throughout their lives.

Let's start with the reasons why companies are cautious about hiring full-time, permanent workers, and why it can be argued that they will be increasingly cautious about doing so in the future.

It's Tough Out There

The first reason is simple: it's a tough economy. Ask any executive, any manager, any worker. Even though the numbers may be good when you ask, even though the stock market may be up and the unemployment rate down, everyone is wary of what happens next, and everyone has an eye on the bottom line. This shouldn't come as a surprise. Although we are a decade on from the recession of 2008, memories are long, and the damage long-lasting.

Even from the vantage point of a strong economy, companies are under tremendous pressure to keep costs (including, or maybe especially, human resources costs) as low as possible. The euphemism often heard these days is "lean and agile," a reference to organizations that do not have a lot of costs weighing them down. In practical terms, this translates to keeping payrolls in check, or at least as efficient as possible. These practices aren't particularly new. The U.S. economy went through a recession back in 1921, and at that time the burgeoning Ford Motor Company, headed by the legendary Henry Ford, was under pressure to improve the bottom line. After toying with measures ranging from price reductions to a gigantic rummage sale that included everything down to the pencil sharpeners, Ford eventually settled on improving productivity and, in particular, creating a just-in-time delivery system— basically, a method to only receive production inputs as needed and thus reduce inventory costs. As a result, he was able to operate factories using nine men per car per day, a 40 percent reduction from the previous 15 men.[8]

Companies are doing the same thing these days, but they're skipping the rummage sale: ramping up productivity gets a big assist from newly available technology. Take the energy sector, for example. Starting in 2014, the price of crude oil began to plummet as a result of a perfect storm of factors, including global oversupply. The price of a barrel of oil as measured by the West Texas Intermediate (WTI) benchmark declined from a high of close to US$110 a barrel in mid-2014 to under $30 a barrel in early

2016—a fall of 75 percent. Oil companies scrambled to completely revamp business plans that had been predicated on much higher assumed prices, and as a result, they were forced to lay off thousands of workers. According to PricewaterhouseCoopers (PwC), global oil and gas companies slashed capital expenditures by 40 percent between 2014 and 2016 and let go of 400,000 workers.

By the end of 2016, however, a decision by the Organization of the Petroleum Exporting Countries (OPEC) to cut production had lifted oil prices, and by early 2017, many analysts had come around to believing that a long-term price of around $50 a barrel could be sustained. Workers were optimistic about being called back to work, but their optimism may have been premature. The thing is, as companies had scrambled to cope with the lower oil prices, they'd also worked on becoming more efficient, which meant reassessing their production processes. For example, before the price slide, it took 30 workers to operate a diesel pump in the shale drilling process. By the time those companies restructured, the same function could be done by two people sitting inside a control van, monitoring automated electrified systems.[9,10] As a result, they ended up needing far fewer workers than they had before the price slide.

The good news for the energy sector is that with the technological improvements, many projects can apparently be profitable with an oil price in the $20 range, a level that would have been unthinkable in the past. Still, companies understand—now more than ever—the need to keep costs down and to continuously improve technology. Not surprisingly, spending on technology rather than workers continues. In its report, PwC suggests that companies continue to examine the role digital technologies can play in improving performance. For example, PwC believes robotics are likely to proliferate in the energy sector as an efficient way to handle complex and repetitive tasks such as connecting pipes and replacing broken machinery, thus reducing labor needs.

We'll discuss the implications of technology in the labor market much more fully in chapter 3; for now, let's simply acknowledge that there is a messy relationship between tech and jobs. Is technology taking away jobs, or are companies seeking out technological solutions when using workers is not ideal, either, because of their cost or because of the nature of the work? Suffice it to say that employers have always looked for ways to keep costs down, and have frequently employed technology as a way to do it. When they are particularly squeezed, they sometimes hasten the search for, and use of, technological solutions. In turn, this means that the demand for workers goes down over the longer term.

Brutal Competition

The second reason why firms are looking for productivity improvements is that global competition is getting more brutal. Emerging-market companies have gained strong footholds, both at home and internationally, for various reasons. They've used technology to achieve efficiencies just as effectively as the large multinationals. Combined with their "home team" advantage, this has allowed many to gain an edge over companies from outside their borders. And in any market, there just doesn't seem to be room for a lot of players. A study of 315 global corporations conducted by Bain Capital found that in major markets, an average of just one or two players earned 80 percent of the economic profit. The increasing success of local firms within emerging countries is a blow to multinationals, which are focused on gaining market share abroad as their own domestic markets stagnate as a result of demographic shifts.

India provides a good example of this dynamic. With a relatively young population (in 2017, the median age in India was 28, compared to 38 in the United States and 42 in Canada[11]), the country is a hotbed of competition in terms of its consumer market, which is both demographically attractive and increasingly affluent. It stands to reason, then, that North American ice cream makers (which do well in young markets), for example, are trying hard to get a piece of the market. And they do have a piece—just not as big a one as they might like. As of 2017, the most successful ice cream brand in India was locally owned Amul,[12] with other domestic brands occupying most of the top-10 list.

But the fall of multinationals can't be blamed on demographics alone. Being big used to be an automatic advantage for companies abroad, one that let them take advantage of their broad purchasing and production powers (what economists call "economies of scale"). But global firms also have big overheads and can be less nimble than smaller ones, and the ability to use technology is something firms of all sizes have recently been able to exploit. As a result, there is a long list of local companies that are gaining on multinationals. In Brazil, for example, local banks Itaú and Bradesco are giving large financial companies a run for their money, and in China, chicken giant KFC is battling to fend off local dumpling brands. According to *The Economist*, as of early 2017, multinationals' share of global profits had fallen to 30 percent from 35 percent a decade earlier.[13]

Taking the Short View

A third strike against traditional employment in North America is the fact that the large, publicly traded companies still standing are now unduly focused on the short term rather than the long view. Publicly traded companies must present results to shareholders every quarter, and meeting financial benchmarks each time is an important indicator in the financial markets. If a company misses an expected earnings-per-share target (typically set by a survey of financial analysts who follow the stock in question), the business media is all over the story, and the firm's stock could tumble quickly. Executive bonuses (which are tied to earnings) are suddenly at risk, and the company itself looks less successful to the world at large. No wonder, then, in this era of activist shareholders, that labor costs are scrutinized so closely. And in accounting terms, an employee is very much a cost (as opposed to an investment), which increases the disincentive to hiring.

Not Your Parents' Corporation

In baseball, three strikes is enough to end your time at the plate, but in the case of employment demand, there are a few more "strikes" to consider. One is the simple fact that the number of big corporations that have traditionally hired large numbers of workers is dwindling. In *Post-Corporate: The Disappearing Corporation in the New Economy*, University of Michigan business professor Gerald Davis details the way that corporations in the United States have been fading over the past couple of decades. The facts are pretty stark. Since 1996, the number of U.S.-based companies listed on the New York Stock Exchange and the Nasdaq has declined by a staggering 50 percent. And the smaller firms that have sprung up face a tough competitive environment. According to research from the Tuck School of Business, the five-year survival rate for newly listed firms has declined by 30 percent since the 1960s.

The reasons for the decline are varied, but at their heart is the fact that the companies we need and are creating today are not the kind that existed in the past. A chunk of new, profitable companies are based in Silicon Valley and are not dependent on going public to raise money. A company like Facebook might ultimately decide to do that, but it spends years accessing venture capital before it goes that route. This doesn't mean that Facebook (or a company like it) does not need workers or employees, but these organizations tend to be structured less formally than traditional corporations, and to hire and fire as they see fit. By Davis's calculations, in 2015 "the combined workforces of Facebook, Yelp, Zynga, LinkedIn, Zillow, Tableau, Zulily and Box were smaller than the number of people who lost their jobs when Circuit City was liquidated in 2009."[14]

Of course, there are many examples of successful new companies that still hire in large numbers. Amazon hired 130,000 workers globally in 2017 alone, bringing its total number of workers to well over half a million. The company keeps posting blockbuster profits, and its chairman, Jeff Bezos, is the richest man the world has ever seen.[15] It's a great news story—except that the success of a company like Amazon has repercussions for a range of other companies within its space.

Amazon—along with other big players such as Apple and Google—is what is known these days as a "superstar" company, one so dazzling that it effectively outshines other players and ultimately drives them out of business. In economists' parlance, having a bunch of superstar companies in a space effectively creates an "oligopoly"—a number of players who on their own would not be able to dominate the market, but who together can set everything from pricing conditions to wages. In a 2018 analysis, Goldman Sachs was perhaps the most conservative voice to raise the alarm on the phenomenon, stating that dominant companies were earning higher profits than ever, but not passing them on in terms of wages. Make no mistake: these companies *are* competitive in terms of wages—in fact, they often pay more than other companies in their industry—but they pay less than they can afford to. Looking at the average increase in the share of industry revenue taken in by the top 20 firms between 2002 and 2012, Goldman estimated that increased market concentration accounted for a 1.5 percent hit to the level of wages since 2002, or a 0.15 percentage point drag to annual wage growth.[16] That may not sound huge, but it's not nothing either. The fact is that industry restructuring—a nice way to phrase it, actually—is costing workers even at the "superstar" firms, who can take or leave what they were offered, while offers at non-superstar firms are clearly waning.

Slower Growth

Finally, looking forward, we have a fifth reason for the trend toward being parsimonious about hiring. Recessions and regular business-cycle fluctuations are no doubt part of the future of North America's economy, but more than that, companies will also be fighting a secular trend toward lower growth. Part of the stellar growth North America saw from the 1950s through the 1980s was due to favorable demographic conditions. With the baby boom generation (born from the late 1940s through the mid-1960s) in their youth, there was a bias toward young households, and a balance between those in their working years and the retired or very young. All things being equal, the speed limit of an economy is equal to the growth of the labor force plus the growth of technological progress. We'll explore this in more detail in chapters 2 and 3, but for now, it's enough to say that for years, that first factor was relatively high. Now, however, with an aging population in North America, demographics are slowing the rate of economic growth.

Think it through: younger people buy more than older ones, and thus power the consumer sector of the economy. (If you doubt that, head into an Ikea on any given weekend. It's packed with twenty- and thirtysomethings, buying Kivik sofas and Billy bookcases to furnish new homes. By contrast, those in their 40s and 50s have housefuls of junk and are holding garage sales on the weekend to get rid of it.) As populations age, the draws on the government coffers get stronger, all while the revenue base that refills them is waning. Sure, companies can be profitable in such a scenario, but they'll have to battle a little harder to do so. And battling harder, unfortunately, does not correlate with hiring more employees.

SUPERSTARS AND EVERYONE ELSE

Given the multitude of reasons to *not* hire traditional employees, it seems somewhat ironic that companies across the spectrum of industries cite difficulty in finding workers as one of their impediments to growth. Ask any company owner, manager, or human resources professional what their biggest issues are and, without doubt, they will tell you that they have trouble finding the right people to fill the positions they have available. This is partly the result of strong economic conditions and partly the result of labor supply (more about that in chapter 2), but some of it can be blamed on what is increasingly becoming a search for "superstars." Employment of one kind or another may exist for many, but the best deals by far are increasingly going to the best of the best—the "superstars," the perfect employees.

This quest for the best can be seen in the fact that labor shortages are not only cited by employers when the economy is hot, but also when it is sluggish. In 2014, the Brookings Institution noted that even though the U.S. unemployment rate was still a relatively high 6.1 percent, employers were complaining about a skills shortage. In fact, two years earlier—when the rate was over 8 percent—manufacturing companies were doing the same, saying that 600,000 jobs were going unfilled. This despite the fact that over the previous 10 years, manufacturers had cut their payrolls by 2.2 million workers.[17]

These apparent worker shortages in times of high unemployment have led to hot debates over whether there exists a "skills mismatch" in North America, and, if so, whether it's a problem that should be remedied. Although there is certainly merit to this argument—not to mention room to improve postsecondary education and training—there is more to the picture. The fact is that companies are increasingly searching for "perfect" workers, ones who can be slotted in "right out of the box," as it were. And once they find those workers, they are willing to pay whatever it takes to get them on board.

Silicon Valley companies provide a classic example of what is happening in the broader economy. In specialized parts of the technology sector, a global war for talent is underway. In fact, for some workers, having the right skills in an area such as artificial intelligence (AI) engineering can give them bargaining power typically reserved for free agents in the National Basketball Association. As the *New York Times* reported at the end of 2017, the average salary for

AI specialists at big tech firms was between $300,000 and $500,000. The most sought-after workers were getting total compensation (including equity) in the range of "single- or double-digit millions over a four- or five-year period" and were able to renew or negotiate contracts "much like a professional athlete."[18]

So, this is one side of the coin: the race to find the perfect employees and pay them accordingly. The other side, though, is a huge reticence to hire anything less than the perfect employee. It all comes back to the competitive economy: there is no time for training, and no time for mistakes. That search for perfection eases every time the business cycle heads up, to be sure, but it is definitely a hallmark of the way business is now done.

THE KALEIDOSCOPE

The last century or so was about employers shuffling labor into an arrangement that worked for them, and for workers to more or less benefit from their choices. Some of those choices and advantages are unwinding, and at first glance, at least, they seem to be doing so in a way that leaves many workers unprepared. Although we may not be going back to pre–Industrial Revolution (or even *Downton Abbey*) days of inequality, we are certainly seeing trends that split the fortunes of workers. None of those trends, however, are set in stone.

Perhaps it is helpful to think of the future of work, and of workers, as something of a kaleidoscope, where the random placement of moving pieces can create any number of pictures. But based on what we know about those pieces, we can be certain that the years—never mind the century—ahead will be a time of radical change.

Going forward, the population trends will be quite different from recent history, which may well give workers a leg up. We also know a few things about technology and the ways that it will change the economy, both in terms of altering our labor needs and in broadening our business horizons. Factor in the ever-evolving global economy and we are left with a new iteration of how we as a society make a living, and how we divide the spoils.

CHAPTER 2

THE DEMOGRAPHIC SWEET SPOT

Bon à s'en lécher les doigts say the signs in the stores, and Quebeckers take the directive to heart. PFK (Poulet Frit Kentucky, known in English-speaking North America as KFC, or Kentucky Fried Chicken) is a popular treat in Canada's French-speaking province, and customers seem to agree that the food is, indeed, finger-lickin' good. As of 2017, the franchise had 64 locations in Quebec, all of which generate steady business from a *poulet*-loving population.

Imagine the outrage and frustration, then, when in the fall of 2017 a PFK in Lévis, Quebec, decided to shut its doors. It was not that the residents of the small town near Quebec City suddenly changed their tastes, deciding to cut down on fat or go vegetarian. Instead, the company found itself with no one to serve its customers. As Richard Hébert, the operations director for Olympus Food (which manages the KFCs in Quebec) put it, it was a "decision of last resort."[19] Despite offering wages higher than the minimum and flexible hours, PFK was drawing a blank in terms of finding workers.

To be sure, Quebec in 2017 was going through a period of hot economic growth, and there was demand for workers across the board. The province has typically had a high unemployment rate, however, so in other years a surge of demand would simply have sopped up the available labor. This time, though, the high demand was hitting a demographic wall. In Quebec, the number of residents between the ages of 15 and 64 fell by almost 1 percent between 2011 and 2016, while the group between 15 and 24, who typically staff fast food establishments, declined by 5.2 percent. In the meantime, the overall population (and presumably its demand for chicken) rose by 3.3 percent, driven by a 19 percent increase in the population over the age of 65. The numbers did not add up, at least for PFK, and so the company drew a blank and closed shop.

It is a story we are going to hear again and again—at least for a while. Quebec as a region is older than the balance of North America, and as such provides a useful leading indicator of what is to come in terms of labor market issues as the population ages. In the extreme, that might indeed mean shuttered doors and a lack of *poulet*; in less dire cases, compromises might be made and solutions found. Any way you look at it, though, a shortage of workers means problems—ones that have not confronted North America for a very long while.

Indeed, we have been waiting a long time for the demographic tsunami, as it is sometimes called, to hit the labor market. Back in the 1980s and 1990s, policy makers were warned that a big shake-up was headed our way when the baby boomers retired. That shake-up is finally happening, and in theory, at least, it should be fantastic news for anyone looking for a job. The story we have been told for decades is that as the baby boomers (that infamous grey ceiling hogging all the great jobs out there) finally, finally, *finally* exit, there will be a shortage of workers. That will be great news for Xers, Millennials, and Generation Z (and, eventually,

Generation Alpha) workers. As they breathe a sigh of relief and move into the corner offices (or wherever), they will be able to dictate their terms of work and be fought over by the corporate sector. Wages will go up, and the unemployment rate will go resolutely down. At last.

Whether that little fairy tale pans out is still up for debate. Every time we've gotten close to it, recessions have cropped up, erasing the demand for workers and taking away their leverage. Looking forward, automation is a separate threat to how many workers we will actually need (more on that in chapter 3). Figuring out the timing—when will robots trump demographics as the dominant economic trend, for example?—is a bit of a challenge, but any way you look at it, demographic change still matters a lot in terms of shaping the future labor market.

This could be the sweet spot for labor: the aging of the population will absolutely have an impact on the way the economy takes shape in the coming decades, and it will absolutely make a difference in how policy is formed. But it might not be a sweet spot that lasts for long: when employers are getting squeezed cost-wise, they can get pretty inventive at finding solutions that improve the bottom line. That makes it doubly important for workers to use this time of demographic advantage to push through as much of their agenda as they can, while they can.

LET'S NOT PRETEND TO BE SURPRISED

It's not exactly a surprise that North American labor-force growth is slowing down: we have known for decades that this was going to happen. If you look at the pattern of births at any given time, you can pretty much predict how many people will be in the workforce 15 or 20 years hence. Sure, that's a bit of a simplification, since it says nothing about immigration or labor-force participation (the proportion of people who decide to pursue labor-force work rather than stay in school full time, stay home with their kids, or retire), but it's a decent starting point, and one that can be adjusted quite easily for other variables.

And there have indeed been ebbs and flows in the number of births in North America. The famous "baby boom" started soon after World War II ended.[20] Economic times were good, and big families were in fashion. In the United States, 3.4 million babies were born in 1946—the most ever in one year, and 20 percent more than the year before. That number continued to rise each year until the early 1950s, and stayed at around 4 million a year until 1964. By that point, there were over 76 million "baby boomers" in the United States, comprising 37 percent of the population.[21] Canada's baby boom came a little later than the one south of the border, and was a little more pronounced. Starting in 1946 and lasting until about 1965, it saw the birth of 8.2 million babies (about 412,000 a year on average), by which time baby boomers were close to 42 percent of Canada's 1965 population.[22] The figures are staggering when compared to today's birth statistics. During the height of the baby boom, the average number of children per woman was 3.7, compared to about 1.7 in recent years.[23]

As the 1960s drew to a close, the baby boom did as well. When the time came for the boomers to have children, boomer women made different choices than their mothers had: they had children later, and they didn't have as many. Take the situation in Canada as an example. In the late 1950s, the "fertility rate" (the average number of children a woman of child-bearing age would have over her lifetime) was close to 4.0. By 1971, that had dropped to 2.1, which is considered "replacement" level, or the level at which population less immigration would not decline. Since that time, the fertility rate has stayed below replacement level.[24]

Between the late 1960s and late 1970s, births slipped to fairly low levels, leading demographers to label the period the "baby bust."[25] To confuse things a bit, the start of Generation X—loosely defined as the generation following the baby boomers—is generally considered to begin in the early 1960s and end in the early 1980s. Despite the overlap, most demographers agree that once the baby boomers started having their own families in large numbers, by about 1980, birth rates rose again. That was the start of the Millennial Generation, so named because the first of them hit adulthood in 2000, in time for the new millennium.

Although there are a couple of other factors at play—immigration being one, and the decision by more women to participate in the labor force being another—it is basically this pattern of births that has shaped labor supply in North America, and continues to shape it today. The surge in births that created the baby boom generation led to years in which the working-age population surged as well. In Canada, the population between the ages of 15 and 64 grew by about 2.4 percent annually between 1961 and 1979. By the 1990s, however, that figure was closer to 1 percent a year; and by 2011, it had fallen to less than 1 percent as the baby boom started to retire and the growth in millennial-aged workers had only begun.[26]

These days, we in North America find ourselves, along with most of the developed world, old and getting older. In 1950, about one in 12 people were over the age of 65; by 2050, this ratio will be one in six. We are in the second half of that 100-year horizon right now, and our world is already a lot less youthful. In Canada and the United States, the median ages of the population in 2017 were 42.2 and 38.1, respectively, up from 26.0 and 28.1 in 1970.[27]

In terms of the labor market, we've gotten used to having swarms of new entrants, and to the economy growing through their contributions. Aided by a rise in the participation of women, labor-force growth surged in the United States and Canada between the 1960s and 1980s. For some years—notably the period in the 1970s when women were entering the labor market in ever-larger numbers—the labor force was growing even more quickly than the population. In the United States, growth in the labor force averaged 2.0 percent per year in the 1970s, 1.6 percent in the 1980s, and 1.2 percent in the 1990s. For the period from 2000 to 2015, that slipped to just 1.0 percent.[28] In Canada, the size of the labor force grew at 4.4 percent in 1979, and managed several years of growth in excess of 3 percent in the 1980s. By 2017, this had fallen to 1.9 percent, and even that was the strongest increase in a decade.[29]

As we approach the end of the second decade of the 21st century, we are at a point where baby boomers are fast exiting the labor force (the youngest North American boomers are in their mid-50s now, while the oldest are well into their 70s), and where the number of millennials becoming labor-force-aged, while still rising, is tapering off. The net result is that the size of the future labor force is not going to grow at the pace to which North America has become accustomed. And if the economy were to continue needing workers at exactly the same pace it has historically needed them, we would indeed have a "shortage" of workers—or, at least, a relative shortage compared to the recent past.

All of this was predicted back in the 1980s, and earlier, when it became obvious that demographics were going to affect the labor force a few decades hence. At the time, the real concern was the retirement of the baby boomers. Put very simply, if there was an ongoing need for a set number of construction workers or teachers or retail workers or physiotherapists, but more were retiring every year than were entering these professions, there would be a "shortage," which was cause for concern. If you do not have enough nurses, how do you provide health care for everyone? If you do not have enough skilled tradespeople, how do you build houses? When those discussions first heated up, predictions suggested that those shortages would put workers in the driver's seat, and that employers would ply them with all kinds of incentives to entice them to sign up or stay put.

But two things happened on the way to those labor shortages. The first was the horrendous world recession that started in 2008. Although it officially ended a couple of years later, its effects continued to be felt for close to a decade. The unemployment rate spiked in the United States and Canada, and every measure of labor market health, from wage growth to the number of long-term unemployed, showed weakness. And there is a very real possibility that demographics cushioned what might have been a much worse story for workers. Had there been more labor-force-aged people looking for jobs, unemployment rates would have been significantly higher, and economic hardship would have been worse.

The second thing that happened was the arrival, in full force, of technology. The possibilities it offered, which had been present and touted for decades, were increasingly embraced by employers. This is a difficult impact to measure, but one that must be taken into account. Consider, for example, the financial sector. While it is absolutely true that the finance sector now employees more people, including more bank tellers, than it did when automated tellers were being introduced to the market, we will never know how many people would have been employed had that technology not been implemented.

Given those two realities—business-cycle fluctuations and the advent of technology—the labor shortage predictions have not played out exactly as expected. At the very least, there has been a delay in them becoming a reality.

Reality is hitting now, however, and examples of occupational labor shortages abound. For example, trucking firms across North America are bemoaning a shortage of drivers, so much so that, by the beginning of 2018, the American Trucking Association reported a need to fill about 900,000 openings. Demographic change is only going to make their situation worse, given that the average age of a truck driver is now 55, or about a decade older than the average in occupations such as construction and manufacturing.[30]

As the situation unfolds, government agencies gamely attempt the difficult task of predicting exactly how many workers will be needed and how many will be available as a way of determining which sectors are going to be in "shortage." For example, in 2017, the government of Canada released projections of the imbalances between labor demand and supply that it thought were likely to exist between 2015 and 2024. The figures concluded that 17 occupations (accounting for 6 percent of total employment) would experience labor shortages during that period. Of these, seven were in health-related occupations, five were in applied sciences, three were in trades and construction, and two were in other occupations. As an example, they cite "psychologist" as an occupation in which there will be more job openings (10,000) than job seekers (8,800) over the period. Given how many variables go into the model, it is an inexact science at best, but it does nail the trends. The reality is that there will be a need for a certain number of workers in each occupation, and for any number of reasons, there will be too few workers in some.[31]

What is not difficult to predict is that health-care occupations are going to be hard-pressed to find enough workers in the future. Nursing is likely to face a double whammy in terms of demographics—an aging population means there will be a burgeoning need for nurses, while an aging nursing workforce means many will be streaming out of their ranks. In the United States, the Bureau of Labor Statistics estimates that, between 2014 and 2022, there will be a shortage (positions in demand versus nurses available) of 1.2 million nurses. By 2016, one million RNs in the United States were already over age 50, which suggests they will be headed for retirement by the mid-2020s or sooner.[32]

Clearly, there are, and will continue to be, worker shortages that cannot be filled quickly and easily; just as clearly, there is a need for workable solutions. Where those solutions come from and how they are implemented can make a major difference in the economy and the work world we end up creating.

IMMIGRATION: THE MAGIC BULLET?

If there are not enough people to do the jobs that need to be done in North America, a simple answer to the shortage would seem to be to bring in workers from elsewhere. Certainly, as some occupational shortages intensify over the next decade, this seems to be a viable method of filling positions. Unfortunately, there is nothing that gets passions riled up more than talking about using immigration as a way to solve labor shortages—regardless of what side of the debate you are on.

Actually, even suggesting that there are, or will be, labor shortages is controversial. Some of those who are against immigration would argue that as long as the unemployment rate is above zero, we have a surplus of labor in North America, and the last thing we need are more potential workers to displace those already here. Others suggest that the problem is not a shortage of labor, but of employers who are willing to pay wages that would attract sufficient workers.

Let's look at each of those arguments in turn. First, where does the unemployment rate need to be before you can say there is a shortage? Well, the number is certainly above zero. Without getting too technical, it's important to understand what economists mean when they talk about the "natural rate" of unemployment, or the "non-accelerating inflationary rate" of unemployment (NAIRU)—the rate at which you pretty much have everyone in the workforce, and below which you would set off an inflationary spiral. There are always some people who have quit their jobs and are looking for new ones, or who are just entering the workforce (such as new graduates). These people may be unemployed, but they may not stay that way for long; they are in transition. Taking these people into account, there is considerable debate as to what unemployment rate is consistent with "full" employment. In the United States, that figure is sometimes put at around 4 percent.[33] In mid-2018, the American economy was at that point, which suggests that a plausible case could be made that labor shortages did indeed exist.

Immigration was a huge issue in the U.S. election of 2016, with then candidate Donald Trump promising to shut down many immigration streams. Genuine labor-force concerns were definitely part of the debate, but so too were concerns about national security should the "wrong" people be allowed to enter. And, of course, emotions and biases also played a role. On the other side of the debate are those who believe we can easily take care of any labor market needs by simply allowing more people into the country. Skills shortages, in this view, are something of a storm in a teacup and could be easily offset.

The second issue, and one that is just as contentious, centers around wages—specifically, around whether immigrants push down wages for the native-born. In the simplest terms, new labor, regardless of where it comes from, is going to depress wages. Conversely, if the size of the labor force suddenly dropped by 80 percent because of a plague, wages for the remaining workers would rise. (That said, if the size of the labor force did drop that much, there would be huge economic repercussions in the form of a drop in production. So it's best not to make the arguments too simplistic.)

According to a survey of the available literature done by the Brookings Institution in 2012, immigrant workers tend to lead to higher opportunities and wages for Americans. To some degree, this is because immigrants and the native-born do not tend to compete for the same jobs, with immigrants often forced to take work that is not the first choice of the native-born, such as on farms or as general laborers. If there is a plausible argument that immigration lowers workers' power, it's related to certain occupational groups, and in particular to those with lower skills and education. That same group, however, is vulnerable to almost every negative workforce trend, including being replaced by automation and the income insecurity that comes from being thrust involuntarily into the gig economy.

What is also clear is that, without immigration, workforce growth in the United States and Canada would be perilously slow. There are really only two ways that economies grow. The first is by having more people working—labor-force growth. The second is through having those people working more efficiently—productivity growth. If a company wants to expand, it can choose between hiring more workers or figuring out a way to increase output using the workers it does have. It is more or less the same for the economy as a whole: to grow gross domestic product, you either need more people or more productivity.

Given the huge reach and potential of automation and robots, you might think that productivity growth has exploded, but it actually has not. Most famously, Nobel Prize–winning economist Robert Solow remarked in 1987 that "you can see the computer age everywhere but in the productivity statistics."[34] Put another way, although the financial markets would suggest that the U.S. economy and tech sector are surging, the benefits of the tech sector are not showing up in the actual productivity figures. In the United States from 2005 to 2017, labor-productivity growth grew at less than half the 3 percent annual rate established from 1995 to 2004.[35] Canada's performance, along with that of many advanced countries, is equally dismal.[36]

There are huge debates as to why productivity growth has been so weak in recent years, with a laundry list of possible explanations floated. Maybe some industries are gaining from computers and some are not. Maybe we are measuring everything wrong. Maybe everything really important that could have been invented (like, say, sanitation) already has been, and coming up with a better smartphone isn't really a game changer. Whatever the reason for the recent sluggishness, it's hard to make the case that we are about to shift directions and will soon see productivity growth surge to 3 or 4 or 5 percent. That said, productivity is a bit of a wild card, and very hard to predict.

Labor-force growth is much easier to wrap one's head around. With the aging of the population, we are already at a point where, in the absence of immigration, labor-force growth in the United States and Canada will soon turn negative. And boosting immigration does not mean that labor-force growth will be particularly strong. In Canada, with its fairly robust immigration program, the government projects that growth in labor supply between 2023 and 2035 will be just 0.4 percent—less than a third of the 1.5 percent observed between 1970 and 2016.[37] In the United States, the Bureau of Labor Statistics in 2016 projected that the labor force would grow by an annual average rate of 0.5 percent between 2014 and 2024, as compared to the 0.6 percent it realized between 2004 and 2014.[38] The tightening of immigration policies since that time makes growth of even that magnitude a stretch.

Even assuming that there was the political will to increase immigration as a way to offset sluggish North American labor-force growth, it is neither a magic bullet nor an unending source of highly skilled labor. The reality is that much of the developed world, and even the developing world, is aging along with North America, and there will be increasing competition for the most skilled and promising workers. Europe is ahead of us in the aging game, and Japan is ahead of it. Indeed, even some of those countries we think of as less developed are growing old.

Take Mexico, for example. Just like its neighbors to the north, Mexico had its own baby boom, one that ended later than it did in the United States and Canada. In turn, this meant that young, low-skilled workers jostled with each other to get jobs at home;

inevitably, some headed for the United States, legally or illegally. It's a story we know well, and it has become part of political lore. The 2016 U.S. presidential campaign was won partly on the basis of then-candidate Donald Trump promising to build a wall between the United States and Mexico in order to reduce the number of illegal immigrants.

But, as was outlined in a paper by economists Gordon H. Hanson, Chen Liu, and Craig McIntosh of the Brookings Institution, demographics may be nullifying the need for the wall.[39] As they see it, between the early 1980s and the mid-2000s, there were lots of reasons for migration from Mexico (and elsewhere in Latin America) to the United States. The U.S. economy was strong, and for those seeking relatively low-paying work, there was not a huge amount of competition from the U.S.-born population, a situation at odds with their circumstances at home. Around the time that the last recession hit the United States, however, the undocumented population in the country began to decline by an average of 160,000 a year between 2007 and 2014. Economics, the authors believed, just hastened a story that was already unfolding as a result of demographics. As they looked forward (using population projections from the United Nations as well as historical migration data), the picture they came up with for the next 30 years looks almost like the inverse of the last 30—no wall required.

The dwindling supply of young labor in the post-baby-boom era is being mirrored in many countries, including most of Europe, but also in newly industrializing countries such as China. To continue their own industrialization processes, those countries will need to retain their own labor, and perhaps bring in more from other countries. As that happens, attracting the youngest and most skilled workers is going to get harder for North America, not easier.

PUBLIC POLICY CHALLENGES

Whether you want to call the problem we are facing an out-and-out labor shortage or just a need to keep the best labor available and in the market, there are public policy challenges ahead. In the worst case, the one with not enough workers in the market, you get a host of undesirable macroeconomic outcomes. One, as previously mentioned, is a situation where you simply do not have enough workers to keep the economy growing at desired rates. Another is that an ongoing shortage of workers would send wages continuously higher, which, on the face of it, sounds perfectly all right (if you are a worker). Problem is, the rising wages are going to be matched by price increases, which will lead to a whole other vicious cycle that is best avoided. In cases like that, central banks such as the Federal Reserve or the Bank of Canada tend to swoop in and raise interest rates to slow things down, perhaps miscalculating and prompting a recession. Again, a situation best avoided.

Governments that wish to avoid either of those situations have some policy options at their disposal. Japan offers a useful example. The country's demographic situation is dreadful, to put it mildly. By any measure, it is the oldest nation in the world (as of 2018, it had a median age of nearly 47, as compared to 38 in the United States and 42 in Canada).[40] Birth rates are low, immigration has always been discouraged, and the country's working-age population has been declining since 1995.

For women, the choice tends to come down to having a job or having children, but not both: according to a 2015 government report, half of Japanese working women suffer some kind of harassment after becoming pregnant, with one in five actually being dismissed from her job.[41] Blatant discrimination aside, a culture of workaholism (called "karoshi" in Japan) has always discouraged women with children from being in the workforce.

In 2013, in an effort to increase the labor-force participation of women, Japanese prime minister Shinzo Abe launched a program called "Womenomics," which increased parental leave benefits, expanded the number of daycare spaces available, awarded government contracts to companies that employ women, and capped compulsory overtime. To date, the policies have had some success. As of 2017, the labor-force participation rate of women between the ages of 15 and 64 has increased by about one percentage point per year, as compared to less than half a percent in the years before the policies were implemented.[42] Although there are still plenty of things to improve in the Japanese economy and labor market, the Japanese experiment does illustrate that government policies can make a difference in changing labor-force participation.

Policies that keep workers in the labor force longer are also a potential solution to the problem posed by demographics. Doing away with a mandatory retirement age (as the United States and Canada have done) is one way to try to retain older workers, while ultimately leaving it up to them to determine whether they wish to continue working. Raising the age at which workers can get government pensions is a much less friendly way to keep people in the workforce.

A ROLE FOR BUSINESS

Although we tend to focus on government solutions when it comes to these issues, businesses have an equally important role to play. Businesses, after all, have a direct stake in attracting needed workers, and perhaps they are best able to craft the policies that will let them do just that. The problem, however, is in creating a somewhat broader mindset than we traditionally see at times when labor is plentiful. When unemployment is high, companies can afford to pay less than they might otherwise; they can also afford to not think too hard about benefits and things related to "work-life balance" (a phrase that it is generally folly to say out loud during recessions). In those times, the ideal worker is one who puts in limitless hours, who demands little in the way of flexibility, and who does not question the status quo of working in anything but a traditional model. But as the economy makes some workers harder to find, and the demographic issues are also factored in, a different situation emerges—one in which all parts of the compensation package can be questioned.

We are already starting to see that happen, albeit slowly. In what has been a strong North American economy in 2018, companies seeking workers are frequently coming up short. Finding themselves in a battle to get the workers they need, many are offering both higher wages and other enticements. And so the stories start to trickle in: stories of industries facing worker shortages, and of companies devising creative ways to find and keep them.

Take the situation in Vermont, a U.S. state where livestock apparently outnumber potential workers in some areas.[43] In early 2018, ice cream ingredient manufacturer Rhino Foods made the news as a result of its generous benefit package, which included offering financial education to its workers. After discerning that many of their would-be employees came from a background of generational poverty, the company also devised the Rhino Income Advance Loan, which allows employees to borrow from a local credit union and then pay the money back through payroll deductions.[44] And that's in addition to regular benefits, of course; as the website says, "Our benefits include all of the usual stuff—medical/dental/ vision/ life insurance—and a Resource Coordinator to assist you with obstacles in your path, an on-site body mechanic specialist to help you with those small aches and pains, and an owner we call the Big Cheese."

What is significant about the Rhino example is that the company's need for workers is strong enough that they are now including perks for workers who might once have been considered "marginal." You can see a similar phenomenon underway in Hawaii, where a shortage of workers to harvest coffee beans is causing so much consternation that the Department of Labor is looking into programs that would allow farm laborers to go from commodity to commodity, making them, effectively, full-time workers.[45] Again, these are what might once have been considered marginal workers, the kind you could hire and discard like tissue. That companies and government bodies are thinking of creative ways to keep them around says something about both the state of the economy and the state of the labor supply.

Of course, workers would generally prefer that their employers simply say it with money, and that seems to be happening as well. By the beginning of 2018—a full *10 years* after the global economic crisis—it had become clear that the U.S. and Canadian economies were at a high point in the business cycle, and that workers were in great enough demand that wages could start to rise. Beginning in the fall of 2017, large retailers such as Target and Walmart in the United States made a splash by announcing that they were raising their lowest salaries (in the case of Walmart, from $9 an hour to $10). Others, including Starbucks and McDonald's, quickly followed. Despite the anecdotal evidence, wage gains were actually happening quite slowly on an overall basis, but the die had clearly been cast. Presumably, there is a lot more to come in the way of wage gains as the demographic tsunami swirls. The answer to the question of how far wages rise is anyone's guess. Will these be the years when everyone gets everything on their wish list? The opportunity is there if workers feel like going after it.

Free training could be another benefit of labor shortages. Training is not something that has been popular among North American employers in recent years. It costs money and, unlike other investments, that's money spent on something you might not be able to hang on to. After all, your newly trained employee could decide to take the skills you paid for and head out the door to your competitor. Right now, however, some employers are desperate enough to try it anyway.

Remember the restaurant situation in Quebec? It's not just PFK/KFC that is feeling the pinch. According to estimates from the Conference Board of Canada, if current trends continue, there will be 8,700 unfilled jobs in Quebec's restaurant industry—a lot for a province with a total population of 8.2 million. As a result, some restaurants are taking the drastic step of training their own cooks. In January 2018, the *Montreal Gazette* ran a story about a pricey restaurant near Montreal called Boefish, where desperation has led the company to put a month of training into kitchen hires to teach them to make specific dishes, a move that would not have been made previously.[46]

AN OPPORTUNITY FOR LABOR

As the demographic tsunami builds, a sweet spot for labor's bargaining power seems to be emerging, and it is one that workers would do well to exploit. For years, workers have seen their leverage eroded by everything from business cycles to technology to demographics. While the first two factors may be out of their control, the third is poised to do an about-face in their favor. The coming demographic shift will offer workers the chance to gain more in terms of earning power, as well as an opportunity to shape the work world a bit more to their liking. This opportunity will not last forever: technology will catch up, and business cycles will go into slower phases. Before it is over, however, we—as a society—will have a chance to redesign policies in a way that works well for everyone. Workers can enter into the conversation from a position of relative strength: for the most part, they will be in some demand and have the ability to push their agenda. Once this sweet spot dries up, however, workers will be less in demand,

and policies may well center around ways to stem income losses rather than anything else.

Looking at it in the broadest terms, the "share" of the economy that labor has managed to get has declined over the past decades. One way to see this is to look at the percentage of national income (all the money earned in a country from sources that include households and business) that is attributed to labor. On a global basis, this was more or less steady for decades, until the 1980s. Since then, wages have grown relatively slowly compared to total economic growth, which means that labor's share has been on the decline. According to calculations by the International Monetary Fund (IMF),[47] labor income shares began to trend downward in the 1980s, reaching a trough around 2008. As of 2017, the IMF calculates that they were about four percentage points lower than in 1970. Although some countries, including Great Britain, have seen labor's share increase since then, workers in other countries continue to lose ground. Between 1998 and 2017, the IMF calculates that the latter has been the case in the United States and Canada.

Like others, the IMF blames labor's losses squarely on two factors: technology and global integration. To be sure, technology that can replace the work done by humans makes workers less competitive. And the fact that countries such as China have emerged as global powers whose goods are sold all over the world has been an issue as well. That said, demographics have also played a role, albeit one that is perhaps harder to discern.

When we think of the rise of a country like China, we most often think in terms of their new industrial strength, which is, of course, part of the story. But there is more to it than that. A large part of China's economic success has come about because the demographic circumstances were right. Between 1990 and 2010, the working-age population in China grew from 66 percent of the total population to 72 percent.[48] This rise in ready workers, who competed with each other for jobs and hence kept wages low, fueled the surge in manufacturing that for a while allowed China to maintain double-digit growth rates. By extension, China's favorable demographic circumstances were a negative for workers in countries like the United States and Canada, which lost industrial ground. In turn, this arguably had an impact on workers' wages, which grew slowly or not at all.

Even within North America, demographics put workers in competition with each other and at a strategic disadvantage in terms of labor market power. During the era when the baby boomers were streaming into their working years and women were entering the labor force, employers had their pick of workers. And when the labor-force growth slowed a bit, the global recession ensured that workers could not gain much of an advantage. Relative to demand, there were always a lot of workers, and it was a boon to business.

Now we are headed into a situation where workers should reclaim some of that power. All other things being equal, the coming demographic crisis should be a bonanza for workers, and, at the very least, stop wage inequality in its tracks. In a 2017 report, the Bank for International Settlements (BIS) went as far as to say that, as a result of the slower labor-force growth, "Piketty is history."[49] The reference is to economist Thomas Piketty, who has been one of the leading voices in chronicling the pronounced increase in income inequality over the past decade. As the BIS sees it, slower labor-force growth in China and elsewhere will allow workers to once more gain some ground.

Those "gaining back ground" years are now upon us. Looking 20 or 25 years into the future, automation may close the window, but for now it is open, and workers should take as much advantage as they can, while they can. There are certainly things to improve on in North America in terms of labor market perks for both men and women, and the time has come for workers to bargain, formally or not, and to introduce their agenda. It should probably have happened earlier: had it not been for the depth of the global recession, we might already have seen companies supporting telecommuting and daycare and a whole host of other benefits. Instead, we saw workers' bargaining power actually erode, as evidenced by wages and pretty much every other indicator as well. The years to reverse that are here, and it remains to be seen what workers make of them.

A word of caution: no one is making the case that the years of employment for life with a fat pension at retirement are back. For so many reasons, that scenario no longer makes sense for many companies. And indeed, many people will not be working for a single employer, anyway. But the demographic advantage will provide a bit of a buffer against the realities that automation may otherwise wreak on work and working conditions. Still, whether or not we end up talking about out-and-out shortages of labor, we will certainly be talking about an older and older labor force and a need to make accommodations for those who are indeed available to work.

CHAPTER 3

A ROBOT WALKS INTO A BAR

You don't need to wonder: of course your boss would love to trade you for a robot.

Today's robots—whether they are walking, talking throwbacks to Rosie from *The Jetsons* or disguised as algorithms or technology-driven kiosks—are *smart*. Robo-advisors can pick stocks now, and they don't seem to do any worse than your average broker. Really cool kiosks can help you order your meal deal at McDonald's, and if you don't want the special sauce, they have no problem passing the message on. A robot (named Botlr, by the way) can even deliver your room-service order in one Silicon Valley hotel.

Robots have been making strides in all kinds of areas for years now. Way back in 2011, a supercomputer named Watson defeated a couple of past *Jeopardy!* champions at their own game. Bored with such lowbrow pursuits, he has now moved on to advising the medical staff at the Memorial Sloan Kettering Cancer Center in New York, where he is highly regarded. A more playful but still highly intelligent robot is AlphaGo, a snazzy algorithm that specializes in the Korean game of Go. In 2015, he became the first program to beat a professional player without handicaps. But forget all those two-bit skills: robots can now serve you drinks. That's right—a robot can walk into a bar and replace a bartender.

Drink-serving robots have been around for years, actually. Back in 2013, a robot named Carl made the news by dispensing drinks in a German bar (he could even manage a bit of small talk, although some patrons found his patter annoying). More recently, the Royal Caribbean cruise line has been experimenting with a robot bartender, and in labor-starved Japan, automated drink dispensers can serve up your scotch.

Not one of the aforementioned robots makes microwave popcorn in the break room, ensuring that its odor (tempting or nauseating, depending on who you are) wafts through everyone's cubicle. Not one whines about their job evaluations, or about their co-workers either. None will drink too much at the holiday party and act inappropriately, nor will they march on a picket line, demanding higher wages. It will never occur to any of them to earnestly ask whether it might be possible to adjust their schedule to help them balance work and family. For human workers, they are the competition, and in the decades to come, they will increasingly, and widely, impose their influence. And let's face it: they have it on workers like you in a million different ways, including, increasingly, the cost of employing them.

Given how cool robots are, and how quickly they are expanding their skill set, it's perfectly rational to ask how many jobs will be left for non-robots over the next couple of decades. According to some of the most dire predictions, millions of jobs will disappear wholesale, creating an era in which a large swath of the population wants to work but cannot. Others say it's just more of the same: that this current "age of technology" is no different from any before it, and that we will inevitably emerge with higher productivity and a better standard of living as a result.

Robots are the scary face of it, but what we're really talking about here is automation, and the ways in which it will impact the demand for labor in the decades to come. If you can do things efficiently and cheaply with robots, all things being equal, you do not need as many humans around. That might mean out-and-out replacement of workers, leading to a higher unemployment rate. More likely, though, it will mean that workers, particularly some classes of workers, find themselves at a disadvantage. This could manifest itself in several ways: bouts of unemployment, to be sure, but also as a need to rely on short-term or gig employment, not to mention lower wages than they might have gotten in the past, and ongoing employment and income insecurity. In fact, these things are happening already, and they mask how weak or strong the economy actually is. If one looks solely at the unemployment rate, all may appear to be good with the economy. Looking at the broader picture, however, it is clear that technology is already having an impact on our working lives (and fortunes), and that the trend is only going to intensify.

We are indeed on the brink of an automation-fueled transformation of the economy. Those who argue that this is nothing new are correct, in one regard: humans have been using technology—in the form of machinery—to change their work processes ever since the wheel was invented. What is happening now, however, isn't "just more of the same." Ultimately, the technology we are creating may end up benefiting everyone, but in the short term—which could last for decades—the adjustment costs are likely to be high.

WHY THE LUDDITES WERE WRONG

These days, robots may be our scariest technology, but, truth be told, humans have always had a love-hate relationship with tech. It's understandable, to a degree: machines that can do what humans do are a little frightening to contemplate. The thing is that, over the centuries, humans have maintained the upper hand in this relationship and have been able to harness the machine power to improve everyone's standard of living. Whether we're talking about a whole new field of work in, say, indoor plumbing, or the rise in factory wages that have resulted from automation, technology has arguably always been a good thing for human beings. But this fact—which we would do well to remember—has done nothing to mitigate that love-hate relationship.

Writing in the fourth century BCE, the philosopher Aristotle gave some thought to the role that technology was beginning to play, and the way it was displacing human actions. "If every instrument could accomplish its own work, obeying or anticipating the will of others . . . if, in like manner, the shuttle would weave and the plectrum touch the lyre without a hand to guide them, chief workmen would not want servants, nor masters slaves."[50] If technology gets advanced enough, he was essentially saying, humans would not need to do any work at all. He might have been several centuries early with his observation, but he clearly saw the way things might unfold.

Several centuries later, when industrialization really heated up, serious concerns about technology's impact on jobs were brought forward more aggressively, this time by the Luddites. We'll talk about who and what the Luddites were in a page or two; for now, suffice it to say that they get a bad rap these days. If you do not have the most cutting-edge phone, you might be called a Luddite by someone cooler than you (frequently a teenager, especially if he or she is related to you). It is an insult, a way to say that you are behind the curve on technology and all of its possibilities. The Luddites, though, were on to something about the way that technological progress can leave workers behind, at least in the short term. That said, transformation of the economy is not exactly a new idea. Consider that, prior to World War I, farmers constituted the largest occupational group in virtually all of what we now think of as "industrialized" countries.[51] A hundred years earlier, farming had constituted virtually all "employment" as we know it. The economy has been in flux for a long time, which is something we would do well to remind ourselves of as we head into this next phase of transformation.

From the 18th century through to the present day, we have been through three distinct "Industrial Revolutions."[52] The first began around 1784, when the world was introduced to a host of technologies including the steam engine, the cotton gin, and machine tools, all of which showed up within a period of 50 years. The Second Industrial Revolution started around 1870 and was marked by the development of electricity, the internal combustion engine, running water, and indoor toilets—as well as the concepts of "division of labor" and mass production. The most recent industrial revolution is the one many of us have lived through. Starting roughly in 1969, and arguably continuing right up to today, the Third Industrial Revolution has given us computing power, laptop computers, smartphones, the internet, and mobile technology. (There is a bit of a debate, however, about the importance of this industrial revolution; as cool as it is to have the latest iteration of the iPhone, it does perhaps pale in comparison to having basic sanitation.)

The Luddites showed up during the First Industrial Revolution. They were skilled artisans from the North of England who looked at all of the new machines on the scene and saw trouble. Their claim to fame was their painstaking handwork when making things like hosiery, which started with the artisans building their own custom frames. When the new industrial machinery was introduced, however, the method of making stockings changed. All of a sudden, stockings were being produced by unapprenticed labor using generic "wide frames." Starting in 1811, the Luddites spent a couple of years warning factory owners to remove the new frames; if the owners refused, the Luddites snuck into the factories at night and smashed the frames with hammers. Their methods may have been crude, but their concerns were real enough: If you have these fancy new machines that do my (skilled) job, what exactly is going to happen to *me*?

In actual fact, the concerns of the Luddites were a bit more nuanced than is normally portrayed. What the Luddites were concerned about was not actually technology, which they were fine with, provided it was employed properly by trained workers. What they *did* fear was that factory owners were adopting technology as a quick way to increase profits while also decreasing wages. Their protests were really about their desire to check items off of a wish list that is surprisingly modern: pensions for workers, a minimum wage, and adherence to some kind of basic labor standards.[53] Their fear was not that technology would be a bad thing overall, but rather that it would benefit a few while disadvantaging many.

In a historical context, the Luddites do seem to have miscalculated. As industrialization heated up through the 19th and 20th centuries, there was a huge demand for labor—and with that demand came a significant increase in workers' standard of living. Still, as much as the general working classes of the next couple of centuries benefited from the productivity gains begotten by machines, the actual Luddites and their colleagues may very well have been hurt by the technology. Adjustment processes are painful, and long-term gain for many is sometimes preceded by short-term pain for a few.

Just over a century later, renowned economist John Maynard Keynes picked up the Luddites' concerns. In the 1930s, he started to worry about something called "technological unemployment"— basically, the idea that mechanization would replace humans in the job market. In a piece titled "Economic Possibilities for Our Grandchildren," Keynes observed: "We are being afflicted with a new disease of which some readers may not yet have heard the name, but of which they will hear a great deal in the years to come—namely, technological unemployment. This means unemployment due to our discovery of means of economising the use of labour outrunning the pace at which we can find new uses for labour."[54] In Keynes's view, technological changes were going to reduce the total amount of work available, leaving us, eventually, with an average workweek of about 15 hours—a scenario that has certainly not come to pass.

What *has* come to pass is that technology has afforded workers some huge benefits. From basic sanitation systems that save lives to smartphones that let you contact anyone, anytime (not to mention post a picture of your lunch on the social media platform of your choice), technology has changed the way we do things, arguably for the better. As well as making us healthier and happier, it has made us wealthier as well. A conservative estimate is that the technological advances of the last couple of centuries have made us ten times wealthier.[55] Back in the day, the Luddites lived a pretty grim life—by whatever economic benchmark you want to use to measure it. Shifts were typically 14 hours long or more, six days a week; overcrowded housing was the norm; and sanitation was such that disease ran rampant.[56] Factory workers today, even if they do not live in luxury, are afforded a lifestyle that would have been unimaginable to 19th-century workers. The spoils of technology may have been distributed unevenly over time, but there is no arguing that workers got some of them, and that it was for the good.

THE FOURTH INDUSTRIAL REVOLUTION: IS IT REALLY DIFFERENT THIS TIME?

But how sure are we that technology will continue to be our friend, or at least enough of a friend to continue to grow our economic opportunities? As we approach the third decade of the 21st century, we are, in the words of Professor Klaus Schwaub, chairman of the World Economic Forum (WEF), on the verge of the "Fourth Industrial Revolution," which may end up being the most significant one of all. This revolution is characterized by technologies that blur the lines between the physical, digital, and biological spheres. Although in some ways this seems like just a progression of the Third Industrial Revolution, the WEF makes the point, emphatically, that it is something different.

According to the WEF, there are three key reasons for this difference: velocity, scope, and systems impact. In a nutshell, the Fourth Industrial Revolution is happening at breakneck speed, or "an exponential rather than a linear pace."[57] As a result, it will have an impact on the way every industry, in every country, operates. It is hard to imagine it all, let alone describe the ways it might change our lives, but there is little doubt that the melding of different technologies is happening quickly and raises exciting possibilities. Whether we are talking about genetics, artificial intelligence, robotics, nanotechnology, 3D printing, or biotech, the possibilities seem to be, if not endless, then at least wider than we have experienced previously.

Let's take the financial services industry as an example. One of the ways that this new industrial revolution is manifesting itself here is through the generation of huge amounts of data, along with new methods of using it. One interesting example comes from Chile, where a fintech (financial technology) startup is helping those without bank accounts or credit cards to access small loans. To assist these customers in building a credit history, they are digitizing "alternative data sources"— including utility bills, automotive credit history, census data, and more—to predict whether they are likely to repay a loan.[58] While this approach raises some ethical questions about the harvesting and use of the data, it also raises possibilities, many of them positive.

Another example comes through the use of DNA in apprehending criminals. In early 2018, the media was abuzz about the capture of the "Golden State Killer," a rapist and serial killer who had terrorized California 40 years earlier. Thousands of tips and old-fashioned police work had not brought the criminal to justice, but a new use of technology did. Over the past decade, individuals have gotten interested in tracing their origins through the use of genetic-testing services. If you use such a service and get an analysis, you can then upload your results in an attempt to find long-lost relatives, which is all kind of nifty and good fun. But what police can also do—and, in this case, did—is upload a killer's profile and see if it matches anyone's DNA. If this doesn't lead them to the actual killer, they can then use public and other records to check family members who might fit in terms of age and profile, and seek out examples of their DNA (perhaps from a cup or piece of gum they have thrown away). In this particular case, that path led police directly to a monster who was living quietly in a suburban neighborhood.[59] Many would argue that this was a good use of new technology: having access to widely available DNA samples enabled the California police to do their jobs better and more effectively. And it's precisely that ability that has characterized the adoption of technology through the ages, and ultimately benefited workers.

The problem this time is that we may not be able to count on that relationship—at least not right away. Although even the most ardent believers in the different-this-time argument would agree that *eventually* the gains from technology might show up as an increase in the standard of living, there are reasons to think that the next decades might be a period of very rough adjustment for workers.

In a sense, we've been dodging this bullet for the past couple of decades, as automation has been introduced at a substantial clip without widespread direct layoffs. Banks and airports have benefited from a surge in productivity by using automated tellers and kiosks for tasks that once had to be done entirely by humans. Grocery stores routinely use self-checkout machines. And, indeed, the relics of what was apparently the last industrial revolution—things like word processing and spreadsheet programs—have made a huge difference to productivity. They have no doubt resulted in default unemployment—or, basically, workers who never needed to be hired to do things like type a memo or deposit a check. But all of this automation did not result in mass unemployment. Bank tellers may not spend their time performing exactly the same tasks they did 30 or 40 years ago, but they still exist as the human face of banking. More important, productivity is one factor that has lifted the finance sector and allowed it to employ many more people in higher-skill functions than it did in the days before instant tellers.

Then again, perhaps there are better indicators than the absolute unemployment rate by which to measure the impact of technology. That is, the unemployment rate is the statistic most quoted in the media, and it is easy for people to understand. If you say that the unemployment rate is the lowest that it has been in decades (which, in 2018, was true for Canada and the U.S.), it sounds like things are great for job seekers, and perhaps in some ways they are. That said, perhaps we need to focus on other statistics to get a feel for what is really going on. One metric to consider, for example, is the labor-force participation rate (which, as we discussed in chapter 1, measures the percentage of people who are either employed or looking for work), and, in particular, the significant shift over the past two decades in the labor-force participation rate of prime-aged males. Historically, men between the ages of 25 and 54 have worked for wages, plain and simple. In 1970, their participation rate in the United States was 95.8 percent. By 1990, that had dropped to 93.4 percent, and by 2000 to 91.6 percent. By 2015, it was at 88.3 percent. It is certainly true that, over that period, many young men stayed in school longer, and many men of all ages have acquired partners who allow them to remain at home. (Sadly, there has also been a rise in the percentage of the U.S. population that is incarcerated). However, the reality is that, for many, the job prospects are just not that great: working is not their best option, and, in fact, is such a weak option that dropping out of the workforce seems to be the best alternative. You can see that even more clearly if you look at what has been happening to men with only a high-school diploma (no postsecondary training at all) over the past two decades. As of 2000, 75.1 percent of those men were in the labor force. By 2014, that percentage had dipped to 67.9 percent.[60]

Not surprisingly, the decline in labor-force participation among men has a lot to do with the fortunes of the manufacturing sector. In 1970, more than 25 percent of U.S. employees worked in manufacturing, a figure that slipped to under 8 percent as of 2016.[61] Lots of things happened over that time period, including the rise of China as a manufacturing center. However, according to an analysis from the Massachusetts Institute of Technology, as much as three-quarters of the decline in employment in the past decades can be attributed to a rise in technology.[62] In earlier decades, manufacturing jobs had typically provided those with minimal skills and education with steady wages and benefits and a solid standard of living. The loss of those jobs—with no replacement in sight—has a lot to do with why men have been dropping out of the workforce, frequently by taking early retirement.

Manufacturing is, in a sense, the canary in the coal mine for the rest of the economy. Just as manufacturing substituted productivity gains for workers from the 1980s onward, at this point in economic history, a confluence of industries are apparently finding it to their financial benefit to use machines *instead of* (rather than in addition to) labor. That is the argument made in two recent books by professors Erik Brynjolfsson and Andrew McAfee of the Massachusetts Institute of Technology.[63] Having looked at the growth of incomes, jobs, gross domestic product, and labor productivity for the decades following the World War II, they observed that all metrics were on the rise until around the 1980s. At that time, however, they found that income growth in the United States was not keeping pace with the growth in the economy, and that, more recently, job growth has become quite anemic as well (even accounting for the 2008 recession). It is, in their words, "the Great Decoupling"—in which the two halves of the cycle of prosperity "are no longer married," and economic abundance keeps rising while income and job prospects for the typical worker falter.[64]

Like many others, Brynjolfsson and McAfee believe that the prospects for many workers are about to get worse. Arguing that we are at the dawn of what they call the "Second Machine Age," they predict that some great things are ahead, and that technology will allow us to produce more health care, more education, more entertainment—really more of everything, and in a relatively environmentally friendly way, to boot. At the same time, however, they argue that computers and robots will be able to do many of the basic tasks that workers do. In their opinion, this means it is not a great time to have "ordinary skills." After all, ordinary skills are easily replaceable skills, and in a world where profit margins are thin, replacing things in a cost-effective way is more important than ever. As the global economy gets ever more competitive and robots get ever smarter, a lot of skills are going to look pretty ordinary, and lot of workers are going to look pretty replaceable.

ARE ROBOTS REALLY COMING FOR YOUR JOB?

That the Fourth Industrial Revolution is happening in some form or another is not really up for debate. Nor is the fact that it will cause some kind of disruption in the labor market. The question is, will the disruption it causes be the kind to which we've grown accustomed over the past several decades, or will it be on another scale entirely? On the optimistic side, if robotics and other new technologies cause businesses to change how they operate but ultimately speed up the economy and create new jobs, we could end up seeing entirely new ways of doing things, and new occupations altogether taking shape. A decade ago, no one could have guessed that "app designer" would be a job, or that people could make small or large fortunes if they had enough followers on YouTube. Go back a little further and no one worked at Amazon, Google, or an Apple store either. Change can be scary, for sure, but it can create opportunities as well. The flip side of this scenario comes via the toll collectors who are no longer needed because booths are now entirely automated, or the factory workers who have met the same fate. As much as that is happening in North America, it is happening more quickly and in a more dramatic way in China, where reports suggest that some factories have already replaced 90 percent of their human workforces with robots.[65]

Unfortunately, there is no way to accurately predict the future and, not surprisingly, no consensus on just how much havoc the Fourth Industrial Revolution might cause. Any estimate has to make some assumptions, many of which are based on past experience and may or may not prove to be relevant. Accordingly, although there have been some comprehensive recent attempts at quantifying job loss connected to the Fourth Industrial Revolution, even the authors of those studies would agree that they are dealing with a moving target. To be sure, a tight labor supply is cushioning many of the negative impacts, and in fact, the decision of Chinese factory owners (among others) to use automation rather than humans is a direct result of labor being scarce and, therefore, expensive. Given that reality, the "best" outcome of such automation is that it erodes the wage advantage that those scarce humans might have had. The worst outcome is that those jobs simply disappear.

The World Economic Federation, in its January 2016 document *The Future of Jobs,* predicts that industrialized countries will lose an estimated five million jobs as they are taken over by machines. Their report was not compiled based on an economic model, but rather through a straightforward survey of chief human resource officers and other top strategists from companies across nine industry categories from 15 of the largest economies in the world,[66] which, by their estimate, cover 65 percent of the global workforce. In contrast to the prevailing view that blue-collar workers are the most vulnerable to job losses through automation, the respondents to the WEF survey felt that those in white-collar office and administrative roles would be affected the most. On a slightly brighter note, the five million jobs lost are, in fact, a net figure, with job losses put at 7.1 million but with two million jobs gained.[67] The respondents saw the jobs gained as likely to be in specialized "job families" such as "Computer and Mathematical" or "Architecture and Engineering."

The WEF figures are actually very low compared to projections by the Bank of England. In a 2015 speech, the bank's chief economist, Andy Haldane, conjectured that machines could put 80 million Americans and 15 million Britons out of work—or 50 percent of the workforce in each country. His analysis was based on analyzing the probability of automation across a range of occupations and then multiplying that by the number employed in each occupation.[68] Haldane looked only at job loss, not at any potential gains that might spring up as the economy changes.

An intriguing way of looking at the way that robots affect the workforce was published by the U.S. National Bureau of Economic Research in 2017.[69] Examining how robots have affected employment, economists Daron Acemoglu and Pascual Restrepo found that between 1990 and 2007, each new robot added to the workforce meant the loss of between 3 and 5.6 jobs in the local commuting area, and that for each robot added per one thousand workers, wages fell between 0.25 and 0.5 percent. Their analysis found a firm connection between the addition of robots and the loss of blue-collar jobs, particularly those in factories.

Acemoglu and Restrepo's conclusions are interesting, but they are based on history rather than projections of the future. For that, we can turn to another study, this one by consulting giant PwC. In a 2017 study, they found that 40 percent of U.S. jobs are at risk of being replaced by robots by 2030, as are about 30 percent of jobs in the United Kingdom, 35 percent in Germany, and 21 percent in Japan. In their view, the most vulnerable jobs are not those in factories but those in the financial sector.[70]

Others agree that automation will replace jobs in the future, but disagree about how quickly that will happen. A comprehensive study published by the McKinsey Global Institute in 2017 found that most jobs could indeed be automated. However, they concluded that, for the most part, automation would transform jobs rather than eliminate them. In addition, McKinsey concluded that entirely automating jobs would take decades, partly because of the massive investments in technology that will have to occur first.[71]

Then again, businesses seem pretty eager to make those investments. Businesses in North America and throughout the world are facing a tough competitive environment at the same time that input costs are on the rise. As things get even tougher over the next decade, and as the costs associated with robots and technology decline, their use may well intensify if the potential payoff looks good enough.

To get an idea of how this might happen, let's consider those factories in China again. In the spring of 2016, a report that Foxconn (a supplier to Apple and Samsung) had reportedly replaced 60,000 factory workers with robots made waves. The company demurred when asked if that would lead to direct job loss, but the fact is that China is now facing a demographic crisis that is radically altering its business model. Much of the country's economic success over the past two decades came about as the result of a seemingly never-ending supply of young workers who made their way from their villages to find employment in factories. That is rapidly changing. According to the Brookings Institution, in 2010, there were 116 million people in China between the ages of 20 and 24; by 2020, the number will fall by 20 percent, to 94 million, and then to 67 million by 2030.[72] Fewer workers means higher production costs—unless you can find a way around using them. That is why China is at the forefront of the robot revolution, and why other countries with aging populations will, in all likelihood, follow suit in exploring technology's possibilities.

If you want to understand which North American industries are going to be the most eager to use technology to actually replace workers, there are two things to consider. First, as in the Foxconn example, the work has to be replicable by machine, a condition that is rapidly being met for many occupations. Second, the industry has to have an incentive to squeeze the cost of labor as quickly and as forcefully as possible. The industry where both of these conditions are very clearly met is the restaurant industry—and, more specifically, the fast food industry.

During 2015 and 2016, there was a very well-intentioned movement afoot to raise the wages of fast food employees, primarily by raising the minimum wage to $15 an hour. In April 2015, protests took place in more than two hundred U.S. cities to make the case that workers needed a higher wage in order to live. The idea of better pay for those workers won widespread support; the minimum wage and the wages of fast food workers in parts of Canada and the United States were raised. In the short term, that's great for the workers, but there's no arguing that over the longer term it also makes them more vulnerable.

Although fast food companies have certainly used technology to make their operations more efficient from day one, we are arguably now at a very pronounced inflection point for the industry.

You can replace workers, pure and simple, with kiosks and other automations. You can see this in-your-face shift in action at one of the kiosks McDonald's piloted in Canada in 2016, which are now being rolled out across the United States. As easy to use as your smartphone, each kiosk lets you click on what you would like to eat, specify any modifications (no mustard on that cheeseburger, please), and pay. You then pick up the completed order at the counter, which is, of course, still staffed by some workers.

As fun as it is to craft a story with victims and villains, it's actually quite difficult to blame the fast food industry for destroying lives by substituting machines for humans. The companies, after all, are ultimately answerable to shareholders, who are not pleased when profits are squashed and stock prices fall. As well, in an ironic twist, customers of fast food restaurants are often income-squeezed themselves, which makes it difficult for the companies to pass on any cost hikes by raising counter prices without seeing sales fall. That means that whether we're talking about higher prices for beef or higher prices for workers, the companies need to find a way to cope.

It's not surprising, then, that executives at those fast food companies are openly talking about replacing workers with machines. In a 2016 interview with Fox News, Ed Rensi, the former CEO of McDonald's in the United States, said that in light of the new higher wages in the industry, "it's cheaper to buy a $35,000 robotic arm than it is to hire an employee who's inefficient making $15 an hour bagging French fries. . . . It's nonsense and it's very destructive and it's inflationary and it's going to cause a job loss across this country like you're not going to believe. . . . If you can't get people at a reasonable wage, you're going to get machines to do the work."[73] Todd Penegor, the CIO of Wendy's, has also been very vocal on the subject. In 2015, he told investors: "We continue to look at initiatives and how we work to offset any impacts of future wage inflation through technology initiatives, whether that's customer self-order kiosks, whether that's automating more in the back of the house in the restaurant."[74]

Mr. Rensi's remarks are especially interesting, since they touch on another topic: in a hotter labor market, there is a smaller pool of workers from which to choose, and thus it becomes more difficult to get "good labor." That makes the situation created by the new, higher minimum wages that much more difficult to manage. The cost of hiring a worker has risen, but even at that high wage, the companies clearly feel that they are not getting to choose from among the best workers. The reasons for this are varied, but they boil down to supply and demand. In a strong economy, a better-educated worker has a choice of whether to take a service-sector job or go somewhere else. In an economy where no one is hiring, the newly minted English graduate is stuck doling out lattes. Once the economy picks up, he is able to get an internship at a media company, which leads to a junior full-time position, and so on and so forth. That might be a simplistic view (and the newly minted English major may not be good at pouring lattes, anyway), but it stands to reason that that a tight economy with high minimum wages may create exactly the conditions that put workers at risk.

Widening the lens beyond the fast food industry, it's clear that the technology already exists to replace many job functions. The McKinsey Global Institute has noted that 40 percent of U.S. employees are in occupations where at least half of their time could be automated by tech.[75] The list includes retail sales and store cashiers as well as workers who prep and serve food. So, although the next massive shift from workers to technology is likely to come in the fast food sector, it will hardly be the last.

It's not hard to think of other job functions that could be automated sooner rather than later. With driverless cars a tantalizing possibility on the horizon, anyone who drives for a living faces some degree of job uncertainty. Uber drivers have been the poster children for the gig economy and the way that technology has created work, but they are actually very vulnerable to having their livelihoods snatched away by the same technology that enabled them in the first place. As a study by the gig platform Thumbtack recently concluded, "commoditized platforms" such as Uber are susceptible to automation.[76] Someone who wants a drive from their home to the airport is looking for a very simple service. If that service can safely be provided by a driverless car or by a robot, so be it.

As much as it is the workers with the lowest skills who will be vulnerable to losing their jobs, all groups face some risk. In a study published in 2013, researchers Carl Benedikt Frey and Michael Osborne looked at 702 occupations in the United States and concluded that 47 percent of workers were at high risk of having their job functions replaced by automation.[77] In follow-up studies, they saw 35 percent of Britons at risk, as well as about 49 percent of Japanese workers. More recently, a 2016 U.S. study done by White House economists found that, so far, automation has particularly hurt middle-skill Americans such as bookkeepers, clerks, and some assembly line workers, who have ended up with lower wages as a result. Looking forward, however, the study's authors concluded that, while the lowest-wage workers were most vulnerable, workers in many different parts of the labor force would also see their jobs threatened. They believe that those making less than $20 an hour face an 83 percent chance of losing their jobs to robots, while those who earn between $20 and $40 are looking at a 31 percent chance. Those with the highest skills were given the best outlook, with the study forecasting that those who earn more than $40 an hour have less than a 4 percent chance of being replaced.[78]

A slightly more optimistic view comes from the Organisation for Economic Co-operation and Development (OECD), which in 2018 put forth a study that builds on the work of Frey and Osborne. After looking at data across 32 countries, they came to the conclusion that close to one in two jobs will be significantly *affected* by automation. However, by their estimates, only 14 percent (or 66 million across the countries studied) are highly automatable—defined as having a probability of automation of 70 percent or more—while another 32 percent of jobs have a risk of between 50 and 70 percent. That latter group may not face out-and-out unemployment, but they are definitely at a risk of seeing the skills required for those jobs change radically, which could affect the way they are compensated. Researchers also found that there will be a significant disparity between the risks of automation for jobs that require significant education and training and those that require lower levels of education and fewer skills. As a result, they consider the risk of job loss as a result of automation to be highest in the manufacturing and agricultural sectors, and lowest in occupations that require professional training or tertiary education.[79]

POLANYI'S PARADOX

Whatever the figures, there is a credible case to be made that some occupations are less vulnerable to job loss as a result of what Massachusetts Institute of Technology professor David Autor refers to as "Polanyi's Paradox." A philosopher whose work was particularly popular in the 1960s, Michael Polanyi found that there were many things that human beings could do without being able to explain why they were doing them. Because robots need things explained to them before they can do them, it is not likely that they will be able to mimic all human tasks. In health-care professions, for example, they can perhaps diagnose patients, but they cannot discern patients' feelings and interact with them accordingly. As a result, Autor has a so-called non-alarmist view of the future. In his view, machines will boost human productivity quickly enough that there will not be mass layoffs of workers.[80]

Whether he ends up being correct is debatable. Lawyers offer an interesting case study in Polanyi's Paradox. Some of a lawyer's tasks involve interacting with clients and perhaps showing emotions and empathy. Other tasks do not. Remember Watson, the supercomputer that is now dabbling in medicine? He is also studying for the bar exam, apparently, and is likely to pass it this year. That aside, many of the more mundane chores associated with billable hours have already been automated, including poring over legal documents and prior cases. To date, this has culled the number of jobs available for new lawyers and has led to a radical decline in the number of law school applicants. According to data from the U.S. National Association for Law Placement, the employment rate for the class of 2015 was 86.7 percent. Although that sounds relatively high, it is about five percentage points lower than the employment rate for the class of 2007. Keep in mind, too, that law schools are graduating fewer students, with overall figures for 2015 down about 10 percent compared to 2010. The number of jobs that 2015 graduates found was down by three thousand compared with 2014, which is about the same as the drop in the number of grads. Had it not been for that drop, the employment rate would have looked even worse.[81] Going forward, a 2016 survey found that 35 percent of the top managers at law firms figured they would replace some first-year associates with technology, as compared to 25 percent in 2011. As well, half believed that paralegals could be completely killed off by computers.[82]

A really interesting area to watch will be the finance sector. Over the past decade, finance has created a huge number of new jobs in Canada and the United States and has become so important that people sometimes criticize the "financialization" of the economy. But many of the jobs in the industry, including some at higher pay grades, look ripe for takeover by robotics. For example, "robo-advisor" platforms such as Wealthsimple are increasingly become the choice of millennial investors as an alternative to financial advisors. To be clear, robo-advisors are not robots that pick stocks, but automated services that ask users a series of questions (What is your investment horizon? What is your risk tolerance?) and then use an algorithm to come up with a plan that users can tweak as they like. They also provide automated portfolio management services. Fees for use tend to be lower than going through an actual human advisor, which is, of course, a draw to many—including, apparently, BlackRock, the world's biggest money manager. In March 2017, the company announced layoffs, saying it was in the process of overhauling its managed equities business so as to drop fees and rely more on computers—or robots—to pick stocks.

To be sure, there will always be a role for human interaction in finance. After all, you cannot pick up the phone and scream at your robo-advisor when the markets are down and have them reassure you that they've seen this before and things will get better. Clearly, however, the sector is in a state of flux. In a 2015 speech, Antony Jenkins, the former CEO of Barclays, said that banking is reaching its "Uber moment," as technological advances will lead to hundreds of branch closures and a possible halving of people employed in the sector.[83] That prediction comes as fintech reaches new heights. An analysis by Citigroup has suggested that banks will cut as many as two million jobs globally as fintech allows computer algorithms to do work now done by humans.[84]

The net result is that while the lowest-paid workers in all industries may be the first to be challenged by robots and algorithms, they will not be the last. An advertising company in Japan is experimenting with a robotic creative director (no word yet on whether he can drink a martini while coming up with a cool idea). The Associated Press uses technology to write uncredited stories on financial news releases. And a professor at Rice University in Texas has said that even sex workers could find their work threatened by robot replacements. Clearly, as automation comes to the fore—cheaper and more accessible than ever—a new model of who works and when will have to be implemented.

TAKING A WIDE VIEW

Given all of the adjustment costs and the misery that may come with the advent of robots and automation, why exactly are we pursuing them so aggressively? The answer is worth remembering: it's because they increase productivity, and productivity eventually creates good things. The question we have to ask is, who gets those "good things"? In the past, they have been shared widely, which has led to a rise in the standard of living for almost everyone. That did not happen overnight, though: working conditions during the first Industrial Revolution were dreadful, and it is doubtful that workers felt particularly grateful to the technologies that kept them in factories 16 hours a day. And to be sure, those Luddites were concerned about who got the gains from productivity. This time around, we can also identify some clear winners in the technology-use sweepstakes, but perhaps that's not the end of the story. Perhaps we need to look harder to see the wider effects—both good and bad—of technology use on the workforce and the economy.

Take the case of Uber. The company (which, like so many of its ilk in the gig economy space, was not publicly traded as of 2018) is clearly gaining from its business idea. By using apps to control both the demand for and supply of car rides, as well as the payment for them, it has created a very efficient way to provide a service. As well, some new work opportunities have been created for those who drive for Uber, offering them a part-time job with hours they can set according to their availability. All those who drive for Uber and enjoy its flexibility, as well as those who use it, would say that they appreciate its existence, which means that the gains from the new technology are not just accruing to a handful of guys in California, but rather are being shared a bit. Some, however, would claim that the advent of Uber has shut down jobs in the taxi industry, or at least depressed earnings. The company has likely hurt the car rental industry as well, and perhaps even the market for public transit. And if Uber is eventually successful in making its driverless cars work, any job gains will be curtailed.

Then again, if Uber is providing a needed service at a better cost than the alternatives, there is a broader win at stake. If a tourist visiting Las Vegas saves money by taking an Uber from the airport, she has more money to spend in restaurants and clubs. If a company uses Uber to shuttle its employees, and thus saves time and money, it has more resources to invest in everything else. Eventually, that "extra" money presumably shows up in retail spending or in investments that ultimately boost the economy. That's the way it's always been: productivity and profits tend to rise together. That was certainly the case when automation and assembly lines made it possible for automotive companies to produce cars cheaply and profitably, and to employ people at relatively high wages.

There is already some evidence that robots can help rather than hurt workers' prospects. Research done by George Graetz and Guy Michaels for London's Centre for Economic Performance found that between 1993 and 2007, the number of robots in use in U.S. manufacturing rose by 237 percent; at the same time, the U.S. economy shed 2.2 million manufacturing jobs.[85] Similar increases in robots and declines in manufacturing jobs are observable in most developed countries. However, Graetz and Michaels also noted that countries such as Germany, which added more robots, actually saw manufacturing productivity surge, and, as a result, shed relatively fewer workers than countries such as the United States, which employed fewer robots. To be sure, even Germany did not *add* manufacturing workers, but at least there is a glimmer of hope that productivity and employment might once again, eventually, move in the same direction.

Inevitably, we have to accept and embrace the fact that the Fourth Industrial Revolution is in full swing. We are crashing through new frontiers where technology is concerned, and that is exciting. In the very best case, we harness the technology available and use robots to increase productivity and wealth. That, in turn, should allow us to create new processes, new companies, new jobs, and new ways of working. If a robot can check out a backpack left in an airport by a suspected terrorist and potentially save the life of a law enforcement officer, it improves the work a police force can do. If online retailing ends up enticing consumers to buy just as much or more than they did previously, there is potential for companies such as Amazon to keep expanding and perhaps to create high-level jobs in tech and professional areas as they do. This is what has always happened, after all: technology may take away some jobs, but it has always eventually been of overall benefit to job seekers. Maybe it won't be different this time.

But even in that best-case scenario, the next decades are sure to be ones of dislocation for many people. Automation may be great, but it is giving employers options as to how to get work done, options that may lead to fewer employees. Then again, the numbers may never show us that phenomenon at all. In most cases, the story is unlikely to ever be as simple as a robot walking into the bar and replacing the bartender, who then faces a lifetime of unemployment. More likely, the bartender will start driving an Uber and taking a few shifts at the Gap, if he can get them. Maybe his income goes down, and maybe his life changes, but it may never be as cut and dried as him facing out-and-out unemployment. And that is why we need to consider much more than the same old yardsticks that once told us whether things were good or bad in the economy.

CHAPTER 4

THE FRAGMENTED FUTURE OF WORK

Question: What happens when you have cash-strapped businesses, a global economy in turmoil, demographic strains, and a smorgasbord of technology at the ready?

Answer: You cut up work into little pieces and make the traditional job just one way to get the work done.

Make no mistake: we are headed into a future where the work world will be all about fragmentation, where you might get paid by one employer for a bit of work or by many employers for lots of bits of work. It will increasingly be a world of gigs, whether that means making thousands of dollars in the C-suite for a four-month assignment, or making 50 bucks for assembling someone's Ikea bookcase. It will be a world where people get together to work on projects and then disperse again, a world where some string together lots of part-time jobs, hoping to make it to a full-time salary. It will be a world where the door to riches is flung open, and the possibility of walking through is there, but it will also be a world of inequities, where some people will feel shut out of ever making a decent living.

Good, bad, indifferent—make your value judgments, if you want. But the reality is that no matter how you feel, the future is already upon us. The gig economy is alive and well, and the work world is only going to get more gig-ified as we move forward. The economic forces that have combined to make it so have taken hold, and no amount of wishful thinking or legislation is going to turn back the clock.

HOW DID WE GET HERE?

Before we delve into why what's become known as the gig economy has grown by leaps and bounds, it might be good to remember that it is, in fact, nothing new. As we saw in chapter 1, it is the firm that is the anomaly, not gig work. Whether we're talking about cottage industry manufacturing or blacksmiths who worked for everyone in the village, gig work has been alive and well since the beginning of, well, work. For a while there, the pendulum swung away from gig work, but now it's swinging back—and the reasons, by now, should be sounding familiar.

At the top of the list is the fact that companies are always looking for cheaper ways to do things, and splitting up work is one way to spend less. To be clear, we're not talking about splitting up work between a number of people, but rather about splitting it up into tasks that can be done on an as-needed basis. Why hire a full-time systems engineer for one special project when you can just commit to her for the six months the project will take? You don't end up with as many people on your permanent payroll, and you don't need to pay benefits either. Contract work has, of course, been around for years, but in a world still smarting from a decade-old recession, it's more appealing than ever to keep wage costs down.

Next up is demographic change. The aging workforce we read about in chapter 2 is also hastening the adoption of gig work. Older workers may have put off retirement for as long as they possibly could, but many are finally heading for the door. And younger workers are not plentiful enough to make them cheap. That's all well and good when the economy is weak, but it's not acceptable when growth is booming. So, sure, employers may have lots of neat ways to entice employees, but at the same time, they're happy to explore ways to keep their wage bills down.

Not that this is all about large companies—and it's not just large companies that are cheap. We all like efficiency. And yes, technology can give provide it. As we saw in chapter 3, technology creates efficiency when we use an app to hail a ride share, and it makes our lives easier when we peruse the 186,447 results we get when we type "baby blanket" into the search field on Etsy, trying to find just the right gift at just the right price. To be sure, technology is helping the gig economy to explode: it's given us platforms that open up the world and set traditional business models on their heels. In the 1930s, Ronald Coase's "theory of the firm" told us that it made sense to hire a bunch of people and sit them all in one place, ready to work; it cost too much to call them in just when you needed them. But a smartphone in everyone's pocket and apps that let you find labor the same way you find a ride have changed that reality. These days, "workers all in one place" is just one of many options, and it may be far from the best.

It would be so simple—too simple, actually—to say that the gig economy is all about technology, and to reduce it to, say, the Uber model. That is one reality, to be sure, but the gig economy is much more complicated than that. There are gig workers at all skill levels; many of them are thrilled to be where they are, and many are anything but. That's why coming up with one set of policies for gig workers or making blanket judgments about what they want and/or need is not going to serve us well. Like everything about our economic future, the gig economy is a complex, ever-evolving thing. And the more we know about it, the better we can prepare for all of its eventualities.

GOODBYE TO OZZIE AND HARRIET

Ever see a picture of the typical family, circa 1960? There was a mom and a dad and two or three kids. They lived together, ate dinner together, and drove around in a car together. If you happened to be selling ketchup or automobiles or lawn sprinklers, you needed to know what that family wanted in their products, and with good reason: as of 1960, two-thirds of all households in the United States were headed by married couples. But flash forward 50 years and it's a different story altogether. As of 2010, that "traditional" family was present in fewer than half of American households.[86] These days, characterizing the market is a lot more difficult for advertisers, and for everyone else.

The labor market is now in the same boat. Not so long ago, "work" was a place that employees went for eight hours a day, over the course of 20 or 30 or 40-odd years. Now, that simple definition is changing so fast, we can barely compile statistics to explain what's going on. And as we've seen, we're not just moving toward a future where the reality of work is not the one to which we'd grown accustomed: we are already there. In this new environment, we are able to get work done efficiently by calling in precisely the labor we need, precisely when we need it. There is a push by consumers and businesses alike to keep costs down. And there is a generational push— partly from millennials, and partly from their much-older colleagues in the labor market—to control the way they work, as well as where and when.

It's a perfect storm, so to speak, a confluence of factors that have come together to fragment the world of work into a million different parts: full-timers, part-timers, contractors, contingent workers, freelancers—in these early decades of the 21st century, we have them all. For more and more people, work is becoming a series of gigs rather than a full-time job, and that's a reality that will have economic repercussions for all concerned. But they needn't all be negative. Moving the economy forward is about harnessing skills and getting the right people in the right places for a period of time. The fragmentation of the workforce is an efficient way to make that happen; if handled correctly, it could be a good thing for workers as well.

If all of this change seems unsettling—and there's no question that it is—it's worth keeping something in mind: that traditional 1960s family unit never went away; it still comprises a chunk of all households in North America, alongside many other types of families now in the mix. Similarly, a core of traditional workers doing their traditional jobs will always be around; they'll just be part of a fragmented world of work that is changing seemingly by the minute.

THE GIG ECONOMY: DEFINING IT AND COUNTING IT UP

There is no precise, agreed-upon definition of the gig economy, although Investopedia takes a stab at it: "In a gig economy," the website states, "temporary, flexible jobs are commonplace and companies tend toward hiring independent contractors instead of full-time employees. A gig economy undermines the traditional economy of full-time workers who rarely change positions and instead focus on a lifetime career."[87] A gig worker, then, is one who moves between gigs and companies, rather than staying in one place.

Right off the top, this definition is problematic: it suggests that gig workers do not focus on a lifetime career, while non-gig workers do. That's simply not true. Musicians and actors, who work gigs as a matter of course, certainly do have careers. It's just so happens that their careers are not played out in one venue, but in many. The same is true for this new wave of gig workers—a wave that will increasingly include workers in all occupations and industrial sectors.

What is nice about the Investopedia definition, however, is that it does not suggest that gig workers must use an online platform. Too often, people hear "gig worker" and their thoughts turn to Uber drivers. But that narrow perspective fails to embrace the scope of the gig economy. Although online platforms are an efficient way to bring workers to where the work needs to be done, many gig workers do not use them at all. Workers at the top of the skills heap, for example, are more likely to find work through executive search firms than they are through platforms.

So, if the gig economy isn't just about technology, what is it? At its most basic, it's about the move to efficiency that is shaping the broader economy; that is, it's about a time (now) in which workers are able to sell (and buyers are able to buy) bits of their time. As we've discussed, the work world is changing not just because of technology, but because employers need to find efficient ways to get things done. Individuals want to do the same. Uber could not exist if individuals did not want efficient and cost-effective ways to get where they need to go. But individuals also want ways to increase their earning power, and technology gives them a tool with which to do so. The Etsys and Fiverrs of the world, which basically take the services that might have been displayed on a single, hard-to-discover website and make them available for the world to buy, meet their needs. Technology is an amazing tool for all that, but it is meeting a demand rather than simply creating one.

The move to gig jobs is also an offshoot of the "sharing economy" that is also a phenomenon of our times. The sharing economy is more of a mindset than anything else. Embracing the sharing economy means renting Badgley Mischka's black "Louisa" gown for an event ($180 from Rent the Runway, compared to buying it for $1,290) or grabbing a Zipcar when you need or want it, rather than buying your own vehicle. It is about saving money, about putting a lower value on ownership and a greater one on practicality. More and more, we are okay with borrowing and renting what we need—and that applies to getting work done as well as finding a dress for an occasion. Of course, technology is part of what is driving that, but it is not the only part.

Still, some people define gig work as being about working through apps. Some define it as anything other than full-time, permanent work. Others include anyone who has a job, but who also has a side gig. No surprise, then, that depending on what definition you use, you can come up with some wildly differing estimates of just how big the gig workforce actually is. The study quoted in chapter 1 by Katz and Krueger, made a fairly high estimate, suggesting that 57.3 million Americans—or 36 percent of the nation's workforce—are now freelancers. That study, however, uses a very broad definition of nontraditional work and includes those who work on contracts, some of which may be long-term.

Most estimates come in a little lower. One of the more comprehensive reports on the gig economy was done by McKinsey & Company in 2016. After surveying 8,000 people, the management consulting firm found that that up to 162 million people in Europe and the United States (which they estimated to be up to 20 to 30 percent of the working-age population) were engaged in some form of independent work. A different count comes from Intuit (the owner of TurboTax), which in 2017 estimated the gig economy to be about 34 percent of the U.S. workforce, and forecast that it will hit 43 percent by 2020. Intuit is using a fairly broad definition that includes platforms such as Uber and Lyft, as well as workers such as plumbers and electricians, who have traditionally been freelancers.[88]

One of the most quoted figures on freelancing comes from Upwork, which since 2014 has worked with the U.S. Freelancers

Union to produce an annual report called "Freelancing in America." According to their 2017 statistics, 57.3 million Americans (about 35 percent of the total U.S. workforce) are freelancing, and that group contributes $1.4 trillion annually to the economy, an increase of almost 30 percent over 2016. This is a very high estimate, which is perhaps not surprising, given that the study counts everyone who is in supplemental, contract-based, or temporary work, or who has been over the prior year. The website Nation1099.com, which compiles data on freelancing, figures that 60 percent of that 35 percent comprises people who are in traditional employment (contract workers, moonlighters who have another job, and temporary workers), and that the rest are "real" freelancers. In total, this group represents 35 percent of the Upwork estimate (22.7 million), or about 14.7 percent of the total U.S. economy.[89]

Estimates on the size of the gig economy in Canada are harder to come by, but one study by the human resources consulting firm Randstad Canada estimates that "non-traditional workers," including independent contractors, on-demand workers, and remote workers, comprise between 20 and 30 percent of Canada's workplace, and that this figure is headed way up in the near future.[90]

The one thing that all of these surveys agree on is that the number of nontraditional workers is growing—and quickly.

COERCED OR BY CHOICE?

Counting up gig workers is one thing, but in order to understand their impact on the labor force, we need to know more about them and their view of gig work. Do they see themselves as forging a cool new way of making a living, or are they gig workers because they have no other choice?

The McKinsey study is helpful in this regard. It groups gig workers into four main subsets: Free Agents (those who actively choose independent work and derive their primary income from it); Casual Earners (those who use independent work for supplemental income and do so by choice); Reluctants (those who make their primary living from independent work but would prefer traditional jobs); and the Financially Strapped (those who do supplemental independent work out of necessity).[91]

The divisions are a useful way to think about the various kinds of gig workers, and indeed remind us that there is not a one-size-fits-all model of gig work. The Financially Strapped, for example, are not a new trend; in the past, they were most often called "moonlighters." The income-squeezed have always taken second (and maybe even third) jobs to pay for their needs. Possibly, there are more workers in this group now; possibly, as well, technology and the current nature of work are making it easier for them to find those second jobs. This group presumably includes those who take on small gigs through a platform such as TaskRabbit as a way to make a bit more cash, or those who babysit on the side, whether or not they use a site like Care.com to find the work. These men and women are not carrying a banner for gig work or gushing about how happy they are to be freelancers; this is a group that is scrambling for more work to survive.

Unhappily, some traditionally secure and well-paying jobs like teaching now have their share of the Financially Strapped in their ranks. According to a survey from the U.S. Department of Education, as of 2015–16, 18 percent of U.S. teachers took jobs outside of schools as a way to supplement their income, up from 16 percent in 2011–12.[92] The second-job seekers tend to be in states such as Colorado, which are known for paying very low salaries: during a walkout for higher pay in early 2018, one teacher was quoted as saying that she received $31,229 after four years of teaching. The same article quoted a school superintendent as saying, "I go to Home Depot and one of my math teachers is helping me on a Saturday . . . he's there because he's working there."[93] Demographic trends suggest that government budgets will be under pressure for years to come, so it's likely teacher salaries will be as well. That means that teachers, along with many other occupational groups, are likely to stay within the ranks of Financially Strapped gig workers.

Certainly, Casual Earners are the beneficiaries of technology. This is the group that has what we now call a "side hustle," and frequently one that is getting an assist from automation. With the technological advances we have seen in the past decade or so, workers have a huge new reach when it comes to their non-primary "jobs." They can be contacted immediately to do work, and frequently they can do that work without leaving home. They can even run profitable companies from their laptops, right from their local Starbucks. In a more pedestrian mode, they can still take on a few hours *at* that local Starbucks to pay their bills, and many are doing so.

Within the Casual Earners group, we also find the Etsy sellers and Airbnb renters and those who use TaskRabbit to find occasional gigs. You'll find teachers here too. A site called Teachers Pay Teachers encourages the buying and selling of all kinds of educational resources, from lesson plans to quizzes to classroom games. Want to make teaching Shakespeare's *Twelfth Night* more fun? Why not try a *Jeopardy!* PowerPoint game (with categories including Act I, Act II, Act III, Act IV–V, Character Quotes, and Characters)—at $1.50 it's a bargain. Or spend a bit more and get a *Twelfth Night* Unit Plan for $20 (the online ratings show lots of stars). Whatever the value of the merchandise, some teachers have apparently been able to give themselves a raise by selling their wares: according to the site, approximately 12 teacher/sellers have become millionaires, while nearly three hundred have earned more than $100,000.[94]

Both the Financially Strapped and the Casual Earners are sometimes referred to as those who have side hustles. This is nothing new: people have been pursuing their passions on the side for a long time. In fact, perhaps the best example of how to do the side hustle correctly—and, in fact, on a royal scale—comes from the Queen. Since she was a young woman, Queen Elizabeth II has had a keen interest in horses and horse racing. For decades, she's been involved in horse breeding, and has owned and raced horses with lucrative results: according to data from Myracing.com, over the past three decades, she has collected a cool $9.3 million in winnings.[95] That is a second income, of course, since her primary job for most of the past seven decades has been ruler of Britain and the Commonwealth. The horse racing business has been based on a passion, and as luck (and hard work and knowledge and the ability to draw on the right resources) would have it, it has paid off in actual dollars (or perhaps pounds). Although few may manage to make their side hustles as lucrative as Her Majesty has, she is clearly a model many hope to emulate, whether they know it or not.

According to a survey by consumer financial services company Bankrate, as of 2017, 44 million Americans claimed that they had a side gig, which they defined as a way to make extra cash aside from their main source of income. Given that the entire U.S. labor force was around 160 million at the time the survey was taken, that means that about 28 percent of the workforce—nearly one in three—was doing something beyond their primary job. That seems like a huge number, and it is certainly higher than the one that comes out of the 2017 Upwork/Freelancers study. According to that, there were 13 million moonlighters in the United States, and a lot of them—more than a third—were eager to make their side hustle their main gig. It is a trend to watch. As incomes for some groups prove to be inadequate, the side hustle is going to be increasingly important, not just as something fun to do, but as a way to keep the lights on.

Thanks to technology, some side hustlers have indeed been able to turn that secondary income into a primary one. It's not a sure thing, but it's possible: you can sit in your house in Toronto or Wichita or anywhere else and come up with a great product idea. You can make it yourself and sell it to the whole world via Etsy, or you can get it manufactured in China, load it onto Amazon, and sell it there. True, you might find that those banana-leaf mouse pads that seemed so cool to you never sell in the kinds of numbers that will let you quit your day job, but the possibility is there, and that is a heady thing.

But what about the "true" gig workers—the ones who are already using gigs as their primary income, and not just dreaming about a day when that might be possible? The two groups that fit that bill are the Free Agents and the Reluctants. At 30 percent and 16 percent of the total, respectively, they together make up almost half of all gig workers in the McKinsey study. By extension, Free Agents would therefore be 6 to 9 percent of all workers, while the Reluctants would comprise 3.2 to 4.8 percent. While these figures are not insignificant, and are certainly likely to grow, they do suggest that, at this point, the number of people using gigs to make a full-time living is still fairly small.

So, who are they? And what do they think about the way they work? James,[96] 46, is a firm Free Agent. A freelance broadcast audio mixer (colloquially known as "the sound guy"), he has worked in media for 25 years, only six of which were spent as an employee of a large company. He left that job 12 years ago and has not looked back. "I make way more money now than I did then," he says. "And technically, I work less, although there are times when I work nonstop. I can set my own schedule, though . . . for example, I usually take the whole month of October off." When asked if he would ever go back to a full-time job for a large conglomerate, he is very certain of his answer: "Absolutely not. No way. No."

James isn't alone. Study after study finds that freelancers are happier than those in traditional jobs, with McKinsey reporting that as many as 97 percent of contractors are *much* happier than their permanent counterparts.[97] These findings are backed up by Katz and Krueger: they found that, as of 2015, 84 percent of independent contractors preferred to work for themselves, about the same percentage that was reflected in similar surveys from 1995 and 2005.[98]

The Reluctants are in a slightly different boat. Unlike James and his ilk, many of whom have chosen to leave full-time work and embrace the gig economy, Reluctants have had gig work thrust upon them. For the most part, these are not the actors delivering pizza to earn a paycheck, or the Etsy sellers who work in offices during the day, nor are they the plumbers or electricians who have a fairly stable trade but a variety of employers rather than a single source of income. This group would prefer, for example, to take a job as a driver with a cab company, complete with the protection of minimum wages and benefits, but is only able to find work with Lyft, and is left trying to get enough full-time hours to make ends meet. The fact is, this group is being forced into gig work and is not finding much that it likes about it. Unlike the Free Agents, they are not excited that gig work is giving them flexible working hours, and many feel that their compensation is much less than it would be for traditional work. Collectively, they get all of the downsides of the gig economy, and none of the upsides.

Without minimizing the genuine concerns of the Reluctants, it's important to remember that, at 16 percent of all gig workers, they represent only about one in six gig workers. As well, even if the gig economy had never been invented, this is the group that would be having the most difficulty in the overall economy. Someone taking a full-time job they do not want as a Lyft driver is likely someone without a whole lot of options. Perhaps their alternative would be unemployment, or a series of part-time jobs in the retail sector. Or perhaps it would be a short-term contract in a factory, followed by no work for several months, and then by some buffering from the unemployment insurance system.

Automation has contributed to, and will continue to contribute to, their woes. While they may not be out-and-out replaced by a robot, they will likely find the work world a more and more fraught place because of the way that automation can replace basic work functions in many industries. When looking for solutions as to how this group can find its best outcome in the future workforce, many point to some kind of legislative solutions, or to government programs as ways to improve their situations. Although both are paths to explore, neither is going to solve what is, at root, a complex problem. The reality is that we should be striving to ensure that as few people as possible are in this Reluctants group, and that for those who do find themselves in this position, their tenure there is as brief as possible.

FROM FAST FOOD TO THE C-SUITE

Accepting that the gig-ification of the economy is in place, it would be hasty to say that it is simply about the lowest-paid workers who have little choice about where to work. Indeed, some of the fastest growth in gig work is occurring at the very top of the economic pile, in executive placement. That makes complete sense from an economic point of view, since hiring on a gig basis allows those who need to get work done to think about putting the right talent and skills in place, as opposed to putting the right employees in place.

"The numbers work," says Jason Peetsma, head of the executive search firm Odgers Berndtson's Executive Interim Division in Toronto. "When a company requires an executive-level talent—CFO, CEO or CIO—time is of the essence. The average tenure of a C-level executive is 4.3 years, the average business model changes every 18 months, and when companies hire incorrectly, the costs can easily mount to one and a half times the base salary.

Juxtapose this against companies that have access to experienced executive-level talent at similar costs to an 'employee' without any risks or costs. If executed correctly, leveraging this type of talent can have a significant positive impact on a business."

Effectively, the workers who go this route are embracing "portfolio careers" (or are "supertemps," as the *Harvard Business Review* once dubbed them[99]). Sometimes, a portfolio career plays out via "fractionalizing," whereby a company gets someone great for a couple of days a week, which perhaps fits their needs and is all they can afford anyway. Or it can mean they get someone great to fill a gap for period of time, with no future obligations. Given the benefits to companies from going this route, it is no surprise that workers who have the skills to fill high-level slots are in such high demand. One HR interim working in Britain puts it this way. "When I go into a transformation programme as an interim I can bring objective views, I can probe into the history of why things are as they are, and I am also distanced from the day to day issues and internal politics that can affect an organisation's employees. One of my favourite questions will always be 'why do we do things this way?' It can unearth a wealth of information and insight that informs how to communicate and engage with employees in the best way to land and embed the change."[100]

For now, gigs for executives and high-level professionals tend to be in areas where skills are easily transferred from organization to organization. That means executives in areas such as finance, marketing, and human resources, but it also means professionals in a wide swath of industries. At the top of the list are workers in information technology and, in particular, workers in information technology who have cutting-edge, in-demand skills. Software development, for example, tends to be "compartmentalized," which means bits of it can be done on a kind of piecework basis.[101]

In 2018, the website FitSmallBusiness.com examined skills where client billings grew by 200 percent between 2016 and 2017, as well as the hourly rates of hundreds of freelancers in those skill areas from popular gig economy websites Upwork, Freelancer, People Per Hour, Hubstaff, and Guru, with an eye to determining the highest-paying gig economy jobs. Their list is revealing: experts in artificial intelligence/deep learning ($115.06 an hour) are at the top, followed by those with an expertise in blockchain architecture ($87.05) and robotics ($77.46). You can also do okay if you know about ethical hacking ($66.33), cryptocurrency ($65.37), and Amazon Web Services Lambda coding ($51), as well as a host of other specialties within technology.[102]

Even a cursory glance at the market shows that gig work so far tends to be concentrated among those with skills who can command very high compensation (such as executives and IT professionals) and those who do not have a lot of pull in the labor market (such as those who rely on retail or fast food jobs and are hired to fill short-term gaps for a few hours a week or perhaps at a busy time of year). Where there is a gap in gig work is in traditional, mid-level corporate jobs, but even there, it is likely a matter of time. The jobs in the middle part of the market are ones where there might soon be a push to find the right workers (because of demographic pressures) as well as the option to use automation (because it is available, and because it can take away the shortages caused by demographics). Adding a third option for companies—that of using contingent workers or supertemps or freelancers—could meet a multitude of goals, including getting the work done and keeping costs in line. For example, if a company typically hires in-house accountants, but demographics mean that they are expensive and in short supply, one option could simply be to pay more for them. Another might be to use as much technology as possible to get the work done. The third, though, is to buy accounting services as needed, perhaps on a part-time basis or just for specific assignments. As we saw in chapter 3, the same can be done for almost any profession.

BOOMERS AND MILLENNIALS AND EVERYONE ELSE

As much as technology and economics are driving the growth of the gig economy, there is also a strong generational aspect to it. At the moment, our workforce is dominated by three separate generations, and each has reasons to utilize, if not embrace, the gig economy. For baby boomers and Gen Xers, the gig economy represents a buffer between them and unemployment, as well as a way to chase their dreams, both before and after retirement. The millennials' situation is different. Tuition costs are high, meaning that many twenty- and thirtysomethings are burdened with high student debt loads. Housing costs are high, too, particularly in major cities. Some millennials are forced into gig work because companies are shying away from hiring permanent employees. Still, even those who have traditional jobs may have a strong inclination to use the gig economy as a stopgap way to boost their incomes.

Let's start with the more mature gig workers. Numbers-wise, boomers and Gen Xers absolutely dominate the gig workforce. According to the 2016 Field Nation Freelancer Survey, 46 percent of freelancers are baby boomers, and another 43 percent are Gen Xers. Millennials make up only 11 percent of the total. It's not surprising, then, that 54 percent of freelancers have 16 or more years of experience in their chosen field.[103] It makes economic, if not intuitive sense. For freelancers (an important subset of the gig economy), the ability to make a living is about having something of value to sell. That value is frequently accumulated after years spent at more traditional employment. Once the value is acquired, though, the options are increasingly open for those who want to try a different business model.

It makes sense, then, that it is those Xers and boomers at the top of the talent heap who are embracing portfolio careers. Peetsma, the Odgers executive who places high-level professionals, agrees that baby boomers are driving the gig economy. "Our typical executive is male, 51 years old, university educated, with 25 years of experience," he said. "They have climbed to the top rung of their functional vertical as either the head of IT, marketing, human resources, operations, or even the CEO. Many of them tell us their decisions usually started at the end of something or a major milestone being completed. They are either bored, uninspired, frustrated, or any combination thereof and think to themselves that it would be great if the next career move was only doing the things they were passionate about." In the past, that decision might have been a pipe dream, given that companies have always thought in terms of "buying" individuals to do jobs rather than buying skills or talent, but now there are more options on the table.

Executives may have the greatest ability to dip in and out of work that they like, but even workers who are not part of the C-suite are also starting to think more about meaningful work and less about climbing a ladder. Sometimes that feeling manifests itself as a decision to quit a position in finance and look for one in the nonprofit sector, or to keep their current job while volunteering somewhere. Other times, however, the gig economy provides the answer. Baby boomers and Gen Xers who are not happy with their current jobs can take advantage of the gig economy to find different work. There are workers who quit their jobs at big corporations to run dog-walking businesses and do a little babysitting, and in-house graphic designers who decide to go out on their own. Technology makes it easier for them to reach a wide audience, and, in the best cases, they are able to follow their dreams as well as make a living. Of course, sometimes it is about the money. "I can make more driving Uber than I can working in an office," says Julie, a fiftysomething who drives in tourist-heavy Charleston, South Carolina. "I used to be a receptionist and then I tried delivering for Uber Eats on the side. Then I added a weekend when I did Uber, and I made more in two days then I would have spending a whole week in the office. So I never looked back."

Julie may have left full-time employment by choice, but there is no arguing that other older workers are getting shoved into the gig economy through layoffs that leave them unable to find the traditional work that they might actually prefer. Dave, 60, falls into that group. He is not counted as unemployed, and there is no government statistic that captures the disruptions that have recently plagued his work life. "I'd been retained by a cloud-based software firm to do all their marketing and communications work," he says. "I'd done it for seven years and helped the company establish its brand in a crowded field." However, his efforts and those of his colleagues were not enough to keep the company afloat. It ultimately filed for bankruptcy, and he was out of a job.

"I'm 'working' now," he says. "But I've been unable to generate anywhere close to a comparable income. On two occasions I've gotten responses to jobs I've applied to and the enthusiasm on the part of both CEOs—who reviewed my current and past work—was akin to 'Usually I'd wait until we've spoken to everyone, but you seem so perfect that I want to meet with you now!' And then I walked in the door. When it was clear that I did not amass decades of experience without ever leaving my late 20s/early 30s, their enthusiasm vanished like a hummingbird."

Dave knows how to market himself and is taking whatever work he can get, from recording audiobooks to strategy and copy work for friends' companies. It may only be giving him one-third of his old full-time salary, but it is a buffer between him and retirement.

Post-retirement, gigs make even more sense for baby boomers and Xers. As easy as it is to associate millennials with side hustles, baby boomers are actually a more natural fit, and arguably will be the group that most embraces them, both before and after retirement (when the side hustles turn into their primary work). Indeed, if some predictions of income shortfalls for the elderly are correct, then a side hustle (or a part-time job) for those at or nearing retirement makes perfect sense: according to the U.S.

National Institute of Retirement Security, the boomers are likely to be the first generation to find themselves downwardly mobile as they retire. "They're going to go from being near poor to poor," Diane Oakley, the executive director of the institute, told *The Atlantic*.[104] Gigs offer at least a lifeline out of that dire prediction.

Millennials may be the workers most associated with the gig economy, but they have a love-hate relationship with the whole thing. As a group, they are the Casual Earners McKinsey has identified: according to Bankrate, younger millennials are the most likely to have side hustles, with 28 percent reporting a secondary income, and 25 percent of that group saying that the second income earns them more than $500 a month. Happy stories of millennials making money on the side are all over the media: the Etsy seller who finds a huge new market for her jewelry, or the musician who is able to finance his serious work with a lucrative wedding market he sources online. At the same time, there is also a mistrust among many millennials, who seem to think the gig economy is some kind of evil plot directed right at them.

A report out of the United Kingdom by Ursula Huws, a professor of labor and globalization at Hertfordshire Business School, found that young people do not generally work in the gig economy (which in her definition involves online platforms) by choice. For the youngest workers, the gig economy is a part of jigsaw puzzle of jobs that provide enough work to get by rather than get ahead (it should be noted that her sample included many students, so it is not surprising that they are not able to find lucrative gig work). There is a subset of younger workers, though, who fit into the classic McKinsey "cash-strapped" category, some of whom resent being directed to the gig economy to make ends meet. Writing in *Glamour* magazine in May 2018, a millennial journalist described her (half-hearted) efforts to boost her income by using various apps to find work. Turned down for work on TaskRabbit ("Hi Helen," read her rejection, "at this time, we do not have the demand for Taskers in the city and categories you've specified, so we will not be moving forward with your registration"), she eventually snares work walking a dog and helping with a friend's laundry, earning around $100 for a week's worth of effort.

"I've always been skeptical of the gig economy," she says in her summary of the experience. "It creates a fantasy that, if you can profit off your every marketable skill, you can subvert the hardships of my much-maligned, profoundly misrepresented generation . . . millennials are raised to be brutally hard workers, even if some of us (me) are probably doomed to spend the rest of our lives writing jokes online. We deserve better than what the gig economy has to offer."[105] "Gig economy is the mass exploitation of millennials," reads a headline from the *Irish Times*.[106] "'Sometimes you don't feel human'—how the gig economy chews up and spits out millennials" is another from the British paper *The Guardian*.[107]

Still, popular mythology suggests that millennials are well suited for gig work. Perceived as a generation that knows how to use technology and has scant use for putting in endless hours of "face time" at the office, millennials supposedly would prefer to go from gig to gig, with perhaps a windsurfing trip to Thailand in between. While there may be elements of truth to that characterization, it is also true that millennials are like every generation before them: they aim to buy homes and start families and pay bills. There is a strong argument to be made that they want actual jobs that pay actual money, week after week, and give them traditional benefits to boot. In fact, older workers are more open to contract work than are younger ones. According to a study by PwC, 65 percent of those over the age of 50 say they would like to be independent contractors, about double the percentage of those under 34 who make the same claim. Like the boomers, they may grow into a preference for gig work, particularly when they as a generation get to the point where it compensates them well. At the moment, however, many millennials seem to be crowded into a part of the gig economy that gives them income insecurity, and as a group, many seem to want out.

And what of the next generations? Generation Z (which, within a year or two, will be reaching adulthood) and Generation Alpha (whose members are toddlers now, but within a little more than a decade will be looking for paid work) will be dealing with whatever we shape the gig economy to be. Already they seem like a entrepreneurial group: according to a 2011 study by Gallup, 8 in 10 students in grades 5 through 12 said they wanted to be their own boss rather than work for someone else.[108] The ingredients are there for them to do it, and perhaps by starting with those expectations they will ease into the fragmented future with more grace than some of their elders.

GOOD, BAD, OR INDIFFERENT?

As the gig economy proliferates, it's tempting to put a value judgment on it, to talk about whether it is "good" or "bad." The simple truth is that it's both—in the same way that the arrival of book megastores were good (for their operators and for those who wanted a wide selection of books) and bad (for the operators of small bookstores and those who preferred to shop them), or in the same way that Amazon is good (for those who want to buy books more cheaply and get them quickly) and bad (for all the stores that sell books).

On the "bad" side, it's become apparent that we have the same type of income inequality in the gig economy that we do in the broader economy. Although there are virtually no statistics with which to really analyze this, it seems likely that income disparities between gig workers are even wider than they are for workers at large. Think about it: at the very top of the gig spectrum are superstar musicians and actors, along with a new breed of tech wizards, consultants, and professionals who are now slipping into gig roles as they please. At the bottom is the group that gets more press: the Uber or Lyft drivers, or the TaskRabbit workers who are involuntarily in the gig economy and would like nothing more than to be old-fashioned, salaried, pensionable workers. In the middle are any number of variations on the theme.

The major fear among those who do not support the gig economy is that we are headed back to the pre–Industrial Revolution days of piecework, in which worker benefits were scarce, if not nonexistent. And it is true that, to get worker benefits today, you need to generally be either an employee (who gets company benefits) or a worker who fits the traditional mold and thus is able to access government benefits (such as parental leave). Gig workers frequently do not qualify for either type of benefits, and as we'll explore later, that is a challenge that will need to be tackled as we move forward. And there are other challenges as well, ones that will force everyone to rethink their assumptions about work.

The time for that rethinking is here. It's too late to prevent the explosion that has taken the labor market into a dozen different directions. Pandora's box has been opened, and there's no closing it now. The question, then, is this: How do we move forward in a way that will benefit all concerned?

PART 2

CHAPTER 5

EMPOWERING INDIVIDUALS

It was a chilling image, and an effective one. On March 28, 2018, four coffins were lined up in front of New York's City Hall as part of a protest against ride-sharing companies. Each coffin represented a New York City cabbie; desperate over their financial situation, four had committed suicide in the months prior to the protest. The cab industry had been turned on its head by the advent of ride sharing, and some cabbies were out of ideas as to how to make a living in an economy where the rules had changed.

To be sure, the cabbies' suicides are an extreme example of the unease many are feeling about the upheavals in the labor market, but they make a crystal-clear point: when rules change and norms are upended, stress builds. And stress is toxic for all concerned. So how can we protect workers in the midst of these changes, some of which are already here, and others still to come? There is no single or simple answer. Government and business certainly have roles to play, but individuals need to be empowered as well. And "empowered" is exactly how we should think of it:

armed with the tools to protect ourselves, and to help our children protect themselves, in the midst of a world in transition.

THE ANXIETY IS BUILDING

There's no doubt that anxiety about the new economy is already building. If we require more proof than empty coffins representing cabbies, we need only look at the daily news. Around the world, numerous populist leaders have been elected in the last few years—a trend that has been linked to voter worries about the future, or about loss of status in the economy. In the United States, the 2016 election of Donald Trump as president is at least partially the result of the unease many Americans are feeling about their economic futures, or, as a study published in the Proceedings of the National Academy of Sciences phrased it, their concerns over their cultural status.[109] Ultimately, it comes down to the same thing: rapid changes to the world and the economy are causing anxiety, and that anxiety can create an impulse to support someone—anyone—who says they can stop the clock. And with disruptions from technology becoming more prevalent, and disparities between the haves and have-nots growing ever wider, the political upheaval is almost certainly going to intensify as well. Potential technological changes are front and center when it comes to workplace stressors. A 2017 study from online learning platform Udemy found that 52 percent of employees were more stressed than they had been a year earlier, with the possibility of being replaced by a robot topping the list of reasons why. More specifically, 55 percent of workers said they fear losing their jobs to artificial intelligence and new technologies at some point in their careers, while others worry about having the right skills. These are fairly startling results. Typically, workers experience stress due to things that are in their face right now—a bad manager, for example, or a toxic work environment. The Udemy study reveals that while workers may still be stressed about these things, they are *more* stressed about mythical robots coming to take their jobs.[110]

But what about those who don't need to worry about the robots, those whose jobs are not likely to be adversely affected by technological advances? Turns out they're not immune to stress either. Teachers are a prime example. As we discussed in chapter 4, teaching continues to be regarded as a solid, middle-class profession. However, wages are frequently not rising at a rate that allows teachers to maintain the standard of living that has been typical for the profession. This is a result of wider trends. Across North America, states and provinces are cash-strapped. Legacy issues (such as a need to make good on generous public-sector pension programs that were put in place many years ago) are partly to blame, but crumbling infrastructure in dire need of upgrading is a factor as well. And we can't forget an aging population that pays less in taxes while simultaneously requiring more health services, which requires some shuffling as far as government resources go. As a result, "good" jobs in the public service—such as teaching—are getting increasingly less good, and income disparities between those in "traditional" professions and those in areas such as tech and finance are growing. A study by the Brookings Institution made an interesting discovery: teachers are the most stressed in areas of the United States that are experiencing the quickest economic growth—growth that others are benefiting from but that is leaving them behind. Consider, for example, San Francisco, where a tech boom has resulted in dizzying house prices. There, even with salaries in the $80,000 range, many teachers find it nearly impossible to get a foothold in the housing market.[111] The situation is so dire that the city now has more dogs than children, as those with children are increasingly unable to afford to live in the city.[112]

All of this stress is taking a toll on our health. A study published in the *Journal of Social Science and Medicine*[113] found that in geographic areas where there was an increasing risk of automation, the physical and mental health of residents was at risk. What we're talking about here are areas where the main industry is perhaps in a large manufacturing plant, and where technology is slowly being implemented in a way that makes workers uneasy. In such places, researchers tallied the cost of those outcomes as they related to absenteeism and health-care costs. They concluded that in a typical county, the impact of automation-related job-loss risk ranged from $37 million to more than $250 million. And yes, nontraditional or gig economy workers may be especially prone to stress. An annual poll from the U.S. public radio program *Marketplace* and Edison Research found that 41 percent of gig workers said they experienced anxiety around work, as compared to 33 percent of full-time workers.[114]

Clearly, these changes to our traditional notions of work are stressing us out, but is the stress warranted? To understand that, it makes sense to think again of the groups of independent-economy workers identified by McKinsey: Free Agents, Casual Earners, Reluctants, and the Financially Strapped. For our purposes here, we can also add those who are employed but who fear losing their jobs, perhaps to technology but also just perhaps to industrial reorganization. Within that group are the Confidents (those who know that they can get another job or find freelance work), the Worrieds (those who are somewhat concerned about the future but who have some confidence in their ability to navigate it), and the Finger-hangers (those who have a job, but who feel like they're hanging on by their fingertips and worry that if they found themselves out of work, they'd be in desperate straits). Of course, there can be movement between these groups: today's Worried could end up a successful Free Agent in the future, and a Reluctant could become a Confident over time. There is also some overlap, with the Financially Strapped existing in all of the employed groups. Our stressed-out taxi drivers, for example, sit somewhere between employed Worrieds and independent-economy Reluctants, although a day may come when they too consider themselves to be Free Agents.

So, what does this mean in terms of stress? When it comes right down to it, everyone but the Confidents and the Casual Earners (the side-hustlers who are happy to work a regular job and pursue their dreams) is going to be feeling it. The Free Agents will be less likely than the remaining groups to experience overall stress (remember, they typically identify as happier than average), although even they will have stress due to the potentially unsteady nature of their earnings. With this in mind, it would seem that the key to lowering society-wide stress—with all of its personal and economic costs—would be to move as many people as possible into one of these three groups. At the very least, the goal should be to have as few people as possible in the categories of Finger-hangers and Reluctants.

FUTURE-PROOFING

So, how do we do this? Certainly, some responsibility rests with governments and businesses—and we'll address that in chapters 6, 7, and 8—but individuals can also take steps to protect themselves against the turmoil ahead.

One way is for people to pursue skills and careers that will be continuously in demand. Sounds easy, right? Unfortunately not. These days, it's next to impossible to get a straight answer to the question "What jobs will there be in the future?" There's a good reason for that. Wind the clock back 20 years or so and imagine someone telling you that you could make a living—an amazingly good one, actually—as a YouTube star. Your first question would have been "What the heck is YouTube?" With the work landscape changing even more quickly now—and new opportunities and platforms cropping up seemingly on a daily basis—isolating specific jobs or careers to pursue is risky business.

Nevertheless, there are still attempts to predict what the future job market will look like. Government labor forecasters gamely try to do so on a regular basis, and it is at least worth looking at their findings. Using a model that combines demand and supply trends (which are, to a large extent, based on demographics), they regularly publish a list of occupations that will have the biggest numeric increase in employment over the coming decade. The top 15 on their list, as of 2018: personal care workers, food-service workers (including fast food workers), registered nurses, home health aides, software developers, janitors and cleaners, general and operations managers, laborers, medical assistants, waiters and waitresses, nursing assistants, construction workers, cooks, accountants, and auditors. It is an interesting mix, to say the least, and it will almost certainly prove to be inaccurate, for a multitude of reasons.

The problem with the Bureau of Labor Statistics (BLS) list is not so much with its supply side, which is relatively straightforward in that it projects the number of workers who will be available based on demographic trends. Rather, the issue is that its "demand-side" model forecasts the demand for each occupation mostly as a function of the way the general economy is growing, and, to an extent, the way that certain industries will require workers based on the forecasters' knowledge of their needs. For example, the demand for personal care aides—which is probably one of the most accurate projections—is based on the fact that the growing population of elderly people will require more workers who can assist them with their needs. When the BLS tries to forecast the number of laborers needed over the next decade, however, its model is not well positioned to account for the ways in which technology might change the demand for their services.

The supply side of the model is driven by demographics, which, unfortunately, does not make it any more accurate. The predicted demand for, say, construction workers is dependent upon how many are expected to retire over the decade. What the model can't estimate, though, is how technological advances might change the demand for certain workers, or how quickly employers will be encouraged to purchase new technology as workers become hard to find and increasingly expensive. In the construction industry, robots are already being used to lay bricks, and can do so three times as quickly as human workers.[115] It's reasonable to expect that robots will be used more and more in this industry, perhaps not displacing actual workers, but certainly cutting down on the demand for them. According to a study by the Midwest Economic Policy Institute, robots could replace or displace 2.7 million jobs in construction in the United States by 2057. The estimates were partly derived from existing work by McKinsey, which suggests that "unpredictable" physical work in construction (such as roofing) has about a 38 percent chance of being automated, as compared to a 70 percent chance for predictable work (such as the work of operating engineers, which can potentially be replaced by self-driving cars).[116] So, by all means, consult the BLS's projections, but do so with the knowledge that they, and others like them, are not forward-looking enough and reflect the occupations currently in demand because of economic and demographic conditions.

It's All About the Skills

Amid this uncertainty, some "best bets" are emerging—sort of. Anything related to the medical field seems like a good risk, given that the demographics alone suggest a huge demand-side need for those who can meet personal and medical needs. But there's a huge caveat: being a doctor or a nurse in the future could be very different than it is right now. Robots that can haul patients around, disinfect rooms, and perform surgery are already being developed.

To be sure, we still have Polanyi's Paradox at play—human beings do things without being able to say why they do them, which means we continue to have a big advantage over robots. And there's also the fact that robots are not yet at a place where they can make ethical decisions. But there's no question that jobs in health care will be evolving. Someone who graduates from medical school tomorrow may still be working as a doctor two or three decades from now, but the job itself may have changed substantially. The same will be true for the majority of professions. It goes without saying that the evolving workplace will not suit everyone, and will certainly be frightening for those who are anxious about change. For those who develop the right skills, however, the continuous transitions will be more manageable.

The World Economic Forum has given some thought to what those skills might be. After surveying human resources and strategy officers from across a range of global companies, it compiled a list of the top skills that workers will need in 2020 (and presumably onward). Rather than being entirely technical in nature, the list featured a number of "soft" skills. The most-needed skill cited is complex problem solving, followed by critical thinking and creativity. Next up are people management, coordinating with others, emotional intelligence, judgment and decision-making, service orientation, negotiation, and cognitive flexibility. Not surprisingly, the bulk of the skills listed are those that robots distinctly lack.

So, how does one go about getting these skills? Probably not via current education models. Writing for the World Economic Forum, Cengage Learning CEO Michael E. Hansen suggests that higher education is in need of a "Netflix Moment," a point at which the accepted norm is disrupted. He suggests this may come through the use of new digital tools and learning platforms that will supplement existing textbooks and curriculums. But even that could be jumping too far ahead: the first step may just be to acknowledge that these are the skills that are needed and try to incorporate them into curriculums, and for individuals to realize that they will need to develop more than "hard" skills if they want to succeed.

None of which is to say that technological skills aren't important. In their own assessment of the skills that will be needed in the future, McKinsey used models to forecast skill shifts through 2030, concluding that the need for technological skills (such as advanced IT and programming) and social and emotional skills (such as those listed by the WEF) would accelerate. At the same time, they saw the need for basic cognitive skills and physical and manual skills declining over the period. Interestingly, McKinsey makes the point that many of the skills we think of as "soft" (advanced communication or entrepreneurial skills, for example) can be taught in the same way that "hard" skills are. Some people may have more propensity than others for these skills, but learning them isn't out of the question.[117]

It is worth reiterating that, no matter how fragmented the workforce gets, there will still be a core of employees who work for companies in full-time, permanent jobs. The trick for those who want to get and keep those jobs will be to develop the skills that make them attractive long-term employees. We know that in every industry, the most predictable functions are the most susceptible to automation. In retail, for example, self-checkouts are already widely in use, and robots are being trained to stock shelves as well. Amazon's Go stores, the first of which opened in Seattle in early 2018, have no visible employees. And, as we discussed earlier, there will a much-reduced need for workers performing basic functions in manufacturing and even in medicine. At the same time, all of these industries will continue to need workers with advanced skills in both technical and "softer" areas. The employees with both will have the brightest futures.

It should come as no surprise, then, that education is a vital aspect of future-proofing. But we're not talking about the tried-and-true options that got us to where we are today. Getting one degree or going through a specific training program and being set for life is a thing of the past. To truly future-proof, workers will need to embrace the idea of continuous training over a lifetime. While this likely does start with getting that first degree, it will continue with taking a variety of courses and upgrading training, both within and outside of the workplace. In some cases, that may happen at the behest of an employer (more about that later). More often, though, it will have to be self-motivated, with individuals continuously asking themselves what their "next" skill needs to be, and then going out and acquiring it.

The good news is that this type of continuing education can act as a buffer when it comes to the inequalities that will be percolating through the economy. With the projected drop in the need for physical skills, the ability to earn a middle-class living will be dependent on acquiring specialized skills that typically come through education and training. That is a shift from the old model, in which doing something like purchasing a taxi medallion could set you up for life (as it did for generations of drivers before the advent of ride-sharing services). Unfortunately, there won't be a lot of "set you up for life" plays in future, but the prospects will still be good for those who are willing to continuously upgrade.

TAKING CONTROL

"It's just not going to happen." That was the answer given by Troy Taylor, CEO of the Coca-Cola franchise for Florida, at a conference held by the Dallas Federal Reserve Bank in May 2018 that brought executives from various industries together to discuss labor market issues. The question? Whether or not U.S. workers could expect to see broad-based wage gains, such as they had enjoyed for decades, in tandem with higher corporate profits. Taylor also noted that, although he was currently adding employees, the long-term plan was to reduce them as he invested in automation.

"Not going to happen" is a bracing bit of reality. Once upon a time, if a company did well, its employees could expect a rubber-stamp increase in pay; in good times, that would mean an increase that was higher than the rate of inflation. Those days are apparently gone—certainly for nontraditional workers, but also for those who are still employees, even at established blue-chips such as the Coca-Cola Company. John Stephens, the chief financial officer at AT&T, was also on the panel in Dallas. While he admitted that the company did not need as many call-center workers or cable installers as it had in the past, he also noted that AT&T was pushing its employees to take nano-degree programs to prepare them for other jobs, whether with them or elsewhere.[118] This is one way that the skills training needed for the future can take place.

Of course, the very idea that anyone will work for a single company for a long period of time is questionable. The "put in your 50 years and get a gold watch" model is already an anomaly, and it's not coming back. In the economy of the future, shifting between different models of work will likely be the norm—which makes it more important than ever for individuals to take control of their own financial futures.

In an ideal world, we'd already be there. Everyone would save aggressively, starting at an early age, both for retirement and unexpected emergencies. Everyone would invest and be cognizant of their financial situation. Everyone would have all the insurance they need, both for health care and everything else. Unfortunately, with the possible exception of those who retired a decade or more ago—and those who have a stable job with amazing benefits expected to continue long after retirement—pretty much no one in the North American labor market fits that bill. The reality is that, in a world where more and more workers are going to cycle through gigs and jobs and careers, financial planning is going to become increasingly important, and the onus will be on individuals.

Gig workers, especially the Reluctants, are at the greatest risk of coming up short financially. This is the group suffering the most from the end of systems like medallions for taxi drivers and manufacturing jobs that paid stable wages and benefits. And with the retraction of physical and basic-skill jobs, many workers are finding themselves in this category, earning less than their previous jobs paid. A British study of gig workers (defined as those who worked through online platforms) found that 25 percent were being paid less than the minimum wage because of the nature of their jobs.[119] In the United States, a study by Prudential Insurance found that "gig only" workers earn $36,500 per year, compared to $62,700 for full-time employees.[120]

For Reluctants, the best approach is to make their stay in the category a short one by transitioning into something else. While the model of the for-life taxi driver may have been replaced with the Uber driver, for example, the transition doesn't need to stop there. Maybe that Uber driver uses her income to build another business, or as a cushion during the completion of her graduate studies. The government could certainly pitch in on this front with retraining incentives, but in the meantime, it will fall to individuals to have and execute their own game plans.

The same holds true for those working full-time jobs that are less and less in demand. Factory work may still exist, and workers may still find jobs in it, but outside of opportunities with large labor unions, the compensation from those jobs will naturally move down as demand declines. It is a sobering reminder that holding on to "jobs" is not the be-all and end-all—especially when those jobs will pay less and less in inflation-adjusted terms and provide for a standard of living that has not traditionally been the norm. This shift in mindset is a leap for individuals and for governments too. Are we truly getting to a point where we decide we don't want to save a factory because the jobs it provides are probably not going to be that great over the long term? The better idea might be to keep that factory in business, but to help workers adjust to a new reality and to accept the fact that if they want to better their prospects over the longer term, they will need to continuously retrain for different work, either within the factory or in a different workplace or occupation entirely.

Being in control financially will be just as important to nontraditional workers who are well paid—and some are very well paid indeed. Consulting company MBO Partners does a survey of independent work that singles out professionals working on a gig basis. By their count, in 2017 there were 3.2 million "full-time independent" workers in the United States who made more than $100,000 annually, up 4.9 percent from 2016. This group represented nearly one in five of all full-time independents. MBO also found that the average income for full-time freelancers was $65,300, compared to a median household income of $56,516.[121] Echoing the findings of McKinsey and others, MBO noted what they called a "barbell" pattern among independent workers. At one end is a growing group with high skills who can do better working independently than they can as employees; at the other are those who perform "commodity work" by maybe picking up a gig assembling furniture off of TaskRabbit, not by choice. The middle is comprised of workers with less extreme prospects.

While these stats are mildly encouraging—suggesting, as they do, that nontraditional work can be satisfying and financially rewarding—they don't change a basic reality: even highly skilled, well-compensated workers will face periods of income volatility. In fact, income volatility will soon be the norm for much of the labor force. In a 2017 study conducted by Ipsos Research for TD Bank, 37 percent of Canadian adults surveyed said they had experienced moderate to high levels of income volatility over the previous year, with about one-third of that group stating that their income could fluctuate by 25 percent or more each month.[122] Not surprisingly, those experiencing income volatility were challenged in terms of savings and financial planning, with 44 percent of those with high levels of volatility showing low financial health, compared to 28 percent of those with low levels of income volatility. Some consider this volatility to be the "third leg" of the "income stool" in Canada, and suggest that it should be viewed in the same way that we currently look at income poverty and income inequality: as a crisis to be dealt with through public policy and private-sector initiatives.[123]

Income volatility is a complex issue. It can and will affect not just Reluctants, but also those who are happy to be running their own business or working gig to gig. It is a special challenge as well for young people facing a working life that will almost certainly involve nontraditional labor at some point. While it may not be possible to completely offset the challenges of nontraditional work, it is certainly possible to prepare—starting with early financial education and planning.

Protect Yourself

Unless offered through a place of employment, insurance and retirement savings plans are often neglected by those starting out in the workforce—and with good reason. The need just doesn't seem likely, at least not in the short term. However, nontraditional workers and those who work for companies that no longer provide these benefits need to take these matters into their own hands. Buying insurance is easy and cheap when you're young—much cheaper, in fact, than investing in a plan when you're older. And the earlier you start putting money into a retirement savings plan, the more you will benefit from compound interest. Do some research, figure out what works for you, and get started.

Start Saving

Saving for a rainy day, let alone for a down payment on a home or another large purchase, may seem impossible on volatile earnings. Projects come in and pay well, only to be followed by sustained periods where nothing comes in at all—creating a "feast or famine" cycle that is hard to break. Even traditional wages can be too skimpy to make savings easy, especially in the "just starting out" phase. Nevertheless, saving is vital. Setting up an automatic savings plan with a financial institution is one way to protect against the lean times—and a necessity for anyone who wants to live a gig existence, with its built-in ups and downs.

Get Educated

In a best-case scenario, financial literacy education would start no later than high school. But we aren't living in a best-case scenario. In 2015, through their Programme for International Student Assessment, the Organisation for Economic Co-operation and Development (OECD) surveyed financial literacy among 15-year-olds across member countries. They found that U.S. teenagers scored around the average, with 22 percent not reaching the "baseline" of financial literacy, and with just over half having a bank account. Canadian teens scored slightly better, with only 13 percent not reaching the baseline, and 78 percent holding bank accounts.[124]

There were some other interesting differences between the assessments in the two countries. Although both exhibited a scoring difference between those who were socioeconomically advantaged and those who were not, the difference was much more marked in the United States, with 11 percent of the variation associated with status, compared to 7 percent in Canada. Notably, though, even the 25 percent of students in the United States who were most advantaged performed worse than students in the third quartile of socioeconomic status in China.

Assuming that all of those 15-year-olds face future that includes a nice, traditional labor market with stable salaries and benefits for all, there is still clearly a need for better financial education. And the truth is that those students are likely to face anything *but* stability ahead, which makes the need even more pressing. Generation Z teens are arguably going to deal with the least stable job future of any recent generation. Some may not realize it for a while, given that a hot economy and a demographic advantage in terms of baby boomer retirements may strengthen their job prospects in the short term. However, the trends clearly point to plenty of volatility over their lifetimes, which means that preparation now is vital. Luckily, it's never too late to start.

BEYOND THE INDIVIDUAL

Ignoring the very real perils of income volatility will certainly create problems for individuals, but it will also have an impact on the operation of the economy as a whole. If people are not able to establish a stable work and income history, it will be difficult for them to do things we now consider routine—such as successfully applying for a mortgage or a loan. At the extreme, we could have a generation, or generations, of individuals who have not built up much in the way of assets, and who as a result have little protection when their income streams end. It is to everyone's benefit to try to avoid that fate. As a society, we presumably do not want to see poverty grow, both for its own sake and because of the havoc that would result if we let that happen.

In the chapters ahead, we will look at what business and government can do to make it easier for workers in this insecure environment, but it bears repeating that we are headed into an "everyone for themselves" era. That might not be ideal in many ways, but it is the reality—and taking care of one's own financial future should be a priority for all.

WORKING ALONE: A LIFE SKILL

Nothing is more annoying than annoying co-workers, right? They show you pictures of their dogs; they brag about their vacations; they talk on the phone at the top of their lungs to their girlfriends about the weekend, or their real estate agents about the condo they are considering. They unwrap their burritos at lunch and then make noxious-smelling popcorn in the break room at 3 p.m. What could be worse than being around them? Well, maybe *not* being around them. As irritating as co-workers might be, they provide something important: a social connection. Whatever the advantages of working outside of a traditional workplace setup, social connectedness is not one of them—and it turns out that social connectedness is fairly important.

Very little attention is paid to the mental repercussions of an unraveling workplace. That should change. Too many in our society already feel isolated, and it's clear that there are both social and economic costs that go along with that. Loneliness, for example, is now thought to be as detrimental to one's health as smoking a dozen cigarettes a day.[125]

Working without a traditional workforce setup can indeed be lonely. A study by Manta Group found that almost one-third of small business owners feel lonely at work, about double the percentage of non-entrepreneurs who say that they do.[126] The trouble is, work has become one of the last places where people make connections. A lot of the institutions that used to bring people together no longer have the same draws. Nearly two decades ago, in 2000, Robert Putnam wrote a book called *Bowling Alone*, which chronicled and lamented the lack of civic engagement in American life. Americans were moving away from political involvement, he argued, partly because they distrusted government. But Putnam also noted a huge movement away from organizations that used to routinely attract people, including those related to religion, but also labor unions, civic clubs, Rotary Clubs, women's groups—and bowling leagues.

The shift, he eventually concluded, was due to a large extent to technology that made it easier to spend leisure time individually, with television, video, and the internet. Incredibly, Putnam was writing *before* the advent of Netflix, iTunes, or Amazon Prime, which is to say that things have gotten worse—and will continue to do so. Take the workplace out of the equation, too, and the potential for social isolation will only intensify, and we could conceivably be at risk of incurring all kinds of costs, including economic ones.

How do we counteract loneliness? One option is through co-working spaces, a trend that has been flourishing in recent years. According to the organizers of the Global Coworking Unconference Conference, there were 14,411 co-working spaces globally in 2017, a figure they forecast to hit 30,000 by 2022. By that time, those spaces will house 5 million members, up from about 1.74 million in 2017. To an extent, these numbers are skewed by large companies that are buying up the spaces (buying a desk or office as needed can make a lot more sense than committing to huge traditional office spaces). That said, co-working spaces are an increasingly popular choice among many "solopreneurs" who prefer to mingle with others rather than work in isolation.

Walking into the WeWork space in Toronto recently, I was struck by the calm atmosphere, the airy cafeteria, and the free chocolates left out as after-work snacks. On another occasion, after speaking at a conference in Montreal, I was told that the WeWork offices were not available for a tour because they were having a party. Someone familiar with the space wryly told me that it seemed that the WeWork people were *always* having a party. On visits to co-working spaces in other cities, I have often found the same thing—a strong social culture that suggests this is a key reason why people are there. An announcement that a co-working space in Kelowna, British Columbia, was doubling in capacity assured would-be workers that "we'll also have a lot more space to play with when we host fun events like Trep Café, Startup Weekend, Lunch

& Learn, BizCamp, Crafternoon Brews, the annual Christmas potluck, or our occasional foosball tournaments."[127]

Of course, co-working is only one way people can make connections in a nontraditional work world. Bowling leagues and sewing circles may never come back, but book clubs and meet-ups could be their modern-day equivalent. Ask anyone who abruptly loses their job, retires, or becomes a stay-at-home parent without building up a social life outside of work: the transition can be tough. As well as financial planning, perhaps individuals also need to think about "life" planning to avoid the costs of isolation, whether that means creating their own book club, starting a meet-up group, or just regularly getting out for a walk.

TAKING RESPONSIBILITY

Even assuming that people make social connections, save their money and arrange benefits, and upgrade their skills, how can we be sure we won't end up with a worst-case scenario—with more empty coffins representing taxi drivers and others who find it difficult to make a living in the work world to come? Certainly, there are those who will find that the future resembles a bad game of musical chairs. Just as they are sure they have a secure perch, their seat will be pulled out from under them. It will not be a game for the weak.

As we've discussed here, preparation is vital—whether through continuous training or personal financial planning or maintaining an open mindset. But we'll also need to change our expectations. We are no longer living in a world where we can sign on the dotted line with one company or buy into one business and assume that all economic conditions will remain static until we retire. We need to accept that those days are gone and learn how to be more nimble. Yes, business can do more to help—governments too. But counting on them to step up may not be the best strategy. Ready or not, we are heading into an age of individual responsibility—and it will be up to us to make the correct decisions for ourselves and our families.

CHAPTER 6

THE CONSTANT CURATION

Worker shortages, a ton of competition, taxes that are not getting lower, and technology spending that's required just to keep up. Oh, and a bunch of stressed-out workers to manage, some of whom you may not even see that often—and some of whom may be robots. Who knows what kind of attitude *they're* going to cop? Fun times, right?

As we saw in chapter 5, it may not be easy to be a worker in this brave new world, but being a manager isn't going to be a walk in the park either. The coming years look to be a time of "constant curation" for North American businesses, at least when it comes to their workers. Continuously, managers will have to choose the right mix of technology and human beings to meet their needs. Attracting and retaining the required talent will be a challenge when everyone else wants crackerjack people too—and wants them at a time when the demographic trends are throwing a wrench in the works. Even more trying, though, will be the continuous need to effectively reassess the employee mix. With not all skill sets in demand, difficult decisions about how to retrain workers—or perhaps release them—will be a major issue in the years to come.

In this new, post-automation world, there will be an opportunity—and maybe an obligation—for business to be a leader. Certainly, some of the responsibility will rest with government (as we'll discuss in chapter 8), but some, by chance or by design, will fall to the private sector. This will pose some interesting challenges and opportunities, but ultimately, the way business chooses to deal with the disruption will go a long way toward shaping the new world of work.

A TIME FOR STRATEGIC PLANNING

Having a plan in place regarding talent may not guarantee success, but it is, at the very least, the first step in creating the best possible future workforce. Strategic planning, particularly as it relates to human resources, is nothing new. These days, though, it is becoming critically important. We are headed toward a juncture where companies will need to make tough decisions about how to allocate resources between technology and workers, and decide exactly what workers their organizations require for long-term success. For large companies, simply engaging the human resources department in the process won't be enough. Effective planning will require giving HR a much more proactive role.

Before we go any further, it's worth taking a moment to determine exactly what we mean when we talk about "strategic planning." Businessdictionary.com puts it this way: "A systematic process of envisioning a desired future, and translating this vision into broadly defined goals or objectives, and a sequence of steps to achieve them . . . in contrast to long-term planning (which begins with the current status and lays down a path to meet estimated future needs), strategic planning begins with the desired end and works backwards to the current status."[128] It is a good way to think of things. Ideally, companies should be thinking of where they want to be at some point in the future (presumably, competitive and profitable) and then working backward to ask what they need to do to get to that point. In practical terms, strategic planning tends to involve several steps, often starting with doing a SWOT analysis (strengths, weaknesses, opportunities, and threats), and then working through an action plan that includes budget projections and a framework to evaluate whether goals are being met.

This is the era of talent. As we head into the next decade, strategic plans must include approaches to assembling and managing a workforce that is the right size and composition to best meet the larger goals of the organization. This will be about head count to an extent, but also about so much more. From decisions on whether employees should be allowed to telecommute (yes, again) to grappling with the issue of how many gig workers to employ, many key decisions will need to be made around talent. Some will involve hiring new employees; others will involve letting go of workers who are no longer a fit. And in between those two extremes will be discussions about retraining and redeploying, and finding ways to use technology instead of people. Everything will be in the mix.

The coming decades will be a time in which human resource departments, or at least human resource functions, come to the fore. This has already started to happen, and with good reason. In the years following the recession of 2008–09, no department that was simply a cost center could or should have survived within many organizations. Once upon a time, when "human resources" was little more than a new name for what used to be called "personnel," the departments were certainly considered cost centers—administrative hubs that did not have much to do with strategy. But in this post-recession era, with its pressing need to transform organizations into leaner and more efficient entities, HR's role has changed—and it continues to evolve. In the best cases, these departments are focused on talent in all of its manifestations, which will be crucial to organizations in the very near future.

Indeed, there already seems to be a tacit acknowledgment that talent is one of the most important elements in a company's success. You can even quantify it: one study of 600,000 workers in fields ranging from entertainment to politics found that the workers management defined as "high performers" were 400 times as productive as those defined as "average."[129] This means that a talent strategy, whoever runs it, is a crucial part of strategic planning. In turn, that likely means a reshuffling of HR responsibilities to include functions that perhaps had not previously been considered. Gone are the days when recruitment and benefits administration comprised the department's work. These days, HR departments need to include personnel who are proficient in data management, employee engagement, diversity management, and employee wellness. And given that the future workforce, even at large firms, will include both permanent and contingent workers, there is also a need for someone who can create a strategy for and manage workers in that broader reality. (We will explore the different models of work and what they will mean in terms of management challenges more fully in chapter 7.)

THE WAR FOR TALENT

So, let's presume you've got a top-notch HR department in place, ready to strategize and manage your talent pool well into the future. The question still remains: How do you attract that talent?

If you want the best employees for your organization, get ready to work for them. Get ready to scramble and battle for and bribe and pamper the people who can do the work you want, when you want it. As we've seen, the demographics are against you, but so is the economy. Even in the midst of the worst recession that

North America had seen for decades, companies in the United States and Canada were complaining that they could not find the workers they wanted. It puzzled economy-watchers at the time, but the fact was that companies then and now do not want to spend their money on anything but the perfect employees, with the perfect skills.

The phrase "the war for talent" is often used to describe the work world we're quickly heading into. Coined in 1997 by consulting firm McKinsey, it was picked up as the title of a book by Ed Michaels, Helen Handfield-Jones, and Beth Axelrod, published in 2001. At the time, the term referred to what was becoming—and still is—a very competitive landscape for talented workers. The thesis was pretty straightforward: the companies that will be successful in winning this war will be those with the right, people-focused mindset, as opposed to a particular set of human resources policies.

As we approach the third decade of the 21st century, we find ourselves with a new reality—kind of like the war for talent on steroids, if you will. In this new battle, organizations will not only be competing for employees, but for workers who can swoop in on a temporary basis and perform whatever work needs to be done. And the fight has also gone global. Once upon a time, North America was the dream location for any kind of talent; these days, other countries are entering the race. Consider artificial intelligence (AI). The United States, led by companies like Google, has traditionally been a world leader in the field and has attracted the best of the best employees, rewarding them handsomely for their expertise. Enter China. In early 2018, the Eastern economic powerhouse announced that it would spend about $2.1 billion on an AI industrial park—the first move of a plan to become a world leader in the field by 2030. Eventually, the park is to house 400 companies, each of which will need workers with high-level expertise. Where China will get these workers is anyone's guess: in 2016, the country's information technology industries reportedly needed five million more AI workers than were available.[130] What this means is that Chinese companies are set to aggressively compete with the Googles of the world (which also operates in China), bribing researchers to leave academia or their existing jobs, or thinking of creative ways to recruit the workers they want. That, of course, means Chinese researchers are less likely to leave China, but it also means workers from Asia, Europe, and, yes, North America might find it lucrative to at least put in some time working in this new, well-funded research hub.

Even within North America, cities are gearing up to fight for new business opportunities and, by extension, to attract talent. To see an example of this—and of some amazing creativity—you need only look at the feeding frenzy that occurred when Amazon dangled the possibility of constructing a new, $5 billion company headquarters in a location to be determined. For sheer entertainment value, it's hard to beat perusing the various bids: Stonecrest, Georgia, promised to make Amazon CEO Jeff Bezos its king; in Kansas City, Missouri, the mayor bought 1,000 products from Amazon, and then wrote 1,000 five-star reviews on Amazon.com; New York lit up the Empire State Building in Amazon orange. In dozens of cities and towns across the United States and Canada, Amazon was promised tax breaks, incentives, and the opportunity to name its terms.

The thing is, Bezos and Amazon were not really looking for anything that out of the ordinary: they were looking for talent (Stonecrest did not even get short-listed, despite the promised coronation). Amazon wants to be in a place where it can set up shop and have its pick of elite workers for years to come, whether through nearby universities and colleges or because the city in question is attractive enough that people will stream into the area to live. (In the short term, Amazon probably wants its pick of non-elite workers as well, although it is moving as quickly as possible to automate as many routine functions as possible.) Most of the cities that threw their hats into the ring got this, which is why the bids were quick to point out their proximity to colleges and universities, their educated population bases, and the fact that their communities were absolutely lovely places to buy a house and raise a family. Any sign that a city was not the perfect place to attract talent was played down. Vancouver, British Columbia, for example, intentionally omitted data that would have shown that housing in its area was in extremely short supply and prohibitively expensive, knowing that this could raise a red flag in terms of its ability to attract talent.[131] Whichever city ultimately ends up with the facility will no doubt draw talent into its orbit, creating challenges for other cities and other companies, which will have to scramble even harder to meet their own needs.

And so, let's say it one more time: we are in an era that is all about the war for talent—and that really is the perfect phrase to describe what's happening. This war may or may not be about putting people in specific jobs or job functions. Sure, it might be about hiring genuine talent that will be with a company over the long term—although perhaps in "jobs" that have yet to be invented. Or it could be about attracting the best talent for a short-term gig—to get a specific job done at a specific time. Both are viable ways for companies to build their workforces, and both will be a part of the world of work in the future. What is going to be less of a going proposition—for employer or worker—is the hiring of people in a specific job function with the promise to keep them around, *in that function*, for the long term. That is not going to work for companies or for the economy as a whole: workforce needs are going to be continuously evolving, and we are all going to have to be nimble enough to make that work.

YOU GOTTA WORK HERE

Here's a news flash for anyone who's panicking about their long-term job prospects: companies will still want to recruit and employ traditional full-time workers. Despite the dire headlines we so often see when talking about the future of work, this reality is not at odds with the way in which the work world is evolving. Yes, the gig economy is splitting up work functions, and it's true that many workers will have no choice but to be contractors, but the fact is that the first choice for many companies is to have at least a core of permanent employees who are both cheerleaders and loyalists. Not that they won't hire and fire that team as necessary, but they do want, and will continue to want, to have the right core people in place. And there will be an ongoing fight for that core group.

As we saw in chapter 2, the demographics of the next decade alone mean that, barring a deep, prolonged recession, the pendulum is shifting against companies and toward workers—or at least toward those workers who have future-proofed themselves by cultivating the attributes and skills that the market favors. By and large, that means the group with the most education, the most adaptability, the highest technical skills, and the best soft skills. In the long term, these folk are the least likely to be easily replaced by technology, and will in fact be able to do more with a technical assist. In the short term, however, that pendulum shift favors all workers. From fast food workers to nurses to engineers, demand will outstrip supply—for a time.

Given this state of affairs, how can organizations best entice those they really want to join their teams? As always, "say it with money" is a solution. Workers already seem to be getting a collective raise as companies staff up following what was effectively a decade-long recession. Indeed, maybe it is something of a benchmark that, by the beginning of 2018, retail giant Walmart announced that it would be hiking wages for all of its U.S. workers, and that those with two decades of seniority would get a $1,000 bonus as well. Beyond that, however, we are entering an era of bidding wars for the "best" available workers. A 2018 study by management consulting firm Korn Ferry suggests that a global "salary surge" could add $2.5 trillion to annual payrolls around the world. The biggest "wage premium" in their findings would be in financial and business services, where bidding for the best of the best is expected to result in a payout of more than double the premium in the other sectors studied. The estimates by country are staggering: in their view, employers in Hong Kong will face a bill of an extra $40,539 a year per skilled worker by 2030, while Australia is looking at $28,625. Only India, a country where young, skilled workers are on the rise, is expected to escape the surge.[132]

Whether these predictions will ever actually manifest themselves is up for debate. If they do, profitability would be sharply impacted, which suggests there would be a swift move toward technology, retraining workers, or shifting operations away from the areas in which in-demand workers are in the shortest supply. But whatever reality ultimately comes to pass, there is no question that there will be heavy competition ahead, and to an extent, it will have to be paid for by actual cash to workers.

Of course, there is more to life than money—a thought employers should embrace if they want to compete in the war for talent. Benefit packages, it seems, may be a key to an employee's heart, and a way that in-demand workers differentiate between workplaces and decide what constitutes a "good" job. Costco is famous for recognizing this. In 2017, the warehouse store was named America's best employer by *Forbes* and Statista (ahead of Google), and was included in Glassdoor's list of the best places to work. As well as paying significantly more than the competition (including Walmart), the company is known for its benefits package, which is much broader than the retail industry norm. The company also provides "guaranteed hours"—rather than the random hours part-time workers often face—and flexible scheduling; the latter has been credited with Costco's ability keep its turnover rate two-thirds below the industry average.[133]

Vacations may also provide a battleground for companies looking to woo workers. At the moment, North America lags woefully behind other parts of the world, notably Europe, when it comes to providing its workers with time off. According to the Expedia Vacation Survey for 2016, vacation times in areas outside of North America tend to be generous, with the business culture supporting the use of the time allotted. In Spain, for example, workers are given 30 days off per year, and they use all of them. Thirty days is also the norm in Finland, France, Italy, and Germany, and in none of these countries do workers typically use less than 25. It is a very different story in North America. In the United States, workers receive an average 15 days of paid vacation, but take only 12. Canadians do a bit better—they tend to take 14 of their allotted 15 days—but North America clearly has a long way to go to catch up to the European model.[134] Perhaps we'll never get there: in a culture that has always valued face time, taking long vacations has traditionally been incompatible with corporate success. In fact, successful people in North America are sometimes known to brag about how few vacations they take. As the war for talent reaches new heights, however, some or all companies may decide to offer more vacation time.

Of course, employees do need to come to work, so savvy companies are trying to make that experience as pleasant as possible, day in and day out. For example, the design of offices is being constantly rethought (or it should be) as the nature of work evolves. For the past couple of decades, the "open plan" office has been the norm, with a 2018 survey by accounting software company Sage suggesting that 80 percent of workers in the United States work under such a system.[135] The latest manifestation of the factory layout championed by engineer Frederick Taylor in the 1900s, the open plan office is the successor to the cube farms of the 1980s, which were heralded as a way to house as many workers as possible while keeping real estate costs low.

The Sage survey suggests that there are pros to having an open plan office, with 65 percent of workers responding that it promotes collaboration. On the con side, however, open plan offices cause productivity to drop by 15 percent (which seems like a low estimate, given that employees in open plan offices are interrupted every three minutes), and they cause sick days to increase by a whopping 62 percent. Oh, and 54 percent of high-performance employees find them too distracting.[136] Want those high-performance employees? Maybe think about a different way to house them.

The search for the "best" office setup is a work in progress, but tech companies (arguably the type most in need of specifically skilled employees) are ahead of the curve. Apple, with its new spaceship-shaped (or donut-shaped, depending on your point of view) Apple Park corporate headquarters in Cupertino, California—on a lot that is 80 percent green space—has a pretty cool setup. So does Airbnb, which is famous for its meeting rooms themed on places where the company has rental space, including one, the Amsterdam room, with wooden-boat seating. For sheer dazzle, however, it is hard to beat what LinkedIn is offering.

The professional networking site snapped up a $26 billion space in San Francisco in 2016 and has since outfitted it with lounges, coffee bars, a spa, a gym (which holds classes all day, to suit individual schedules), a lending library, a cafeteria that carries several varieties of kombucha, modern art worthy of a first-rate museum, and a "silent disco" where employees can groove to music while wearing headphones.[137] One look at the wall that dispenses fortune cookies, and you'll want to work there.

What most of these new work spaces have in common, in and out of tech, is that they're built around the idea of "activity-based working" rather than an older tradition of having people assigned to specific offices or workstations. The idea is that employees can work in the spaces they choose, whether it's the lounge, a café, or a more traditional workstation. Time will tell whether this works or becomes a massive bust—the open plan office 2.0. Still, just the idea that offices are evolving to meet competing needs (including, obviously, the need to contain real estate costs) is potentially a positive, and the companies that hit on the most appealing configurations may be the ones that are most successful in creating happy, productive employees who want to stick around.

THE BIGGER PICTURE

There's a great story about a visit John F. Kennedy made to the NASA space center when he was president. Seeing a janitor, Kennedy asked the man what he was doing. The man answered proudly, "I'm helping put a man on the moon."[138] It's a beautiful response, one that speaks to the fact that every employee in the organization saw themselves as part of a big, wonderful project that gave meaning to whatever they did each day, even if it was pushing a broom. This same mindset encouraged many who would have ordinarily turned up their noses at such work to flood factories during World War II as blue-collar workers. These men and women were not just working on an assembly line, they were helping to win the war. Company goals may be less lofty these days, but it still pays to let every worker know what their role is in the bigger picture.

At the end of the day, work is not just about bonuses or benefits or even flashy workplaces. Consulting company the Energy Project, in partnership with the *Harvard Business Review*, did a survey of 12,000 mostly white-collar employees to figure out what made people engaged and happy at work (recall that, according to Gallup, only 30 percent of U.S. workers and 15 percent of global workers consider themselves to be "engaged"). The results showed that people are satisfied and productive when four core needs are met: physical needs (through opportunities to regularly renew and recharge at work), emotional needs (through being made to feel valued and appreciated), mental needs (through empowering them to decide when and where to work, and providing the opportunity to focus), and spiritual needs (by making them feel connected to a higher purpose at work).[139]

Companies that meet those needs reap strong benefits. For example, the survey found a nearly 50 percent increase in workers' capacity to work creatively if they took a break every 90 minutes, as compared to those who took no breaks. It also revealed that the more hours workers put in above and beyond the traditional 40 hours a week, the worse they felt. That seems like pretty basic common sense, but in a world where working long hours has become the norm for so many—not to mention a badge of honor—it really is a point worth noting, especially from an employee-retention standpoint.

The "value" issue is important for employees, as measured by both this study and many others. According to the Energy Project, feeling "cared for" by their supervisor and company has a huge impact on employees, with those who say they have supportive supervisors being 1.3 percent more likely to stay with their organizations. Although this kind of assessment tends to elicit eye rolls from managers who see "employee wellness" initiatives as a soft-skill, human resources approach to the workplace, there are hard costs, in terms of financial losses, to companies that don't make their employees feel appreciated. According to a 2017 study, 66 percent of employees figure they would "likely leave their job if they didn't feel appreciated." Interestingly, this is much higher than the 51 percent who said the same thing in 2012, at a time when the economy was significantly weaker and labor was much less in demand.[140] In other words, the tighter the labor market gets, the more employees are likely to jump ship if they feel taken for granted.

With this in mind, it would seem that imparting a sense of "value"—sometimes expressed as "purpose"—is a key concept for would-be employers to consider, perhaps even the most important concept of all. The Energy Project's data suggests that employees who derive "meaning and significance" from their work are three times less likely to change jobs than those who do not. Recruiting firm Hays puts it this way: "Employee engagement was traditionally driven by a good salary and attractive benefits, but today most people see these as a given . . . instead they look at what an organisation is working towards and known for. Crucially, they want to know that, as an employee, they will understand what they are working towards and how they make a difference, which gives them a greater sense of purpose."[141]

This is the approach that NASA apparently got so right back in the early 1960s, and the approach that many companies are apparently getting so wrong today. Some, though, are on the ball. Remember the company I mentioned in the introduction—the one that invited me to host its employee-engagement event? It clearly knew what it was doing in terms of creating a bigger-picture experience for its workers. That it was gathering workers together to talk about their level of engagement at all was a big clue, and it's a strategy more companies would do well to emulate. That said, there are other ways to help employees feel valued, or that they have a sense of purpose. That can happen via specifically scheduled meetings to touch base, or it can happen when managers make it a point to just do so on a daily basis. Either way, constant communication of what the organization is doing—and the employee's specific role in it—can go a long way.

RETRAINING AND RESKILLING—AND MAKING HARD CHOICES

"Why retraining is the new recruiting" reads an article headline on Payscale, the compensation-market website. Off the top, it seems as if the site's take on the issue is going to be somewhat familiar: workers are going to get replaced by technology, so the humane thing to do is to train them for other functions. In fact, Payscale's insight is a lot less altruistic. What it and other firms that specialize in recruitment conclude is that the talent crunch cannot be managed just by looking for new workers—at least not efficiently. Retraining is going to be important, especially when you consider that younger workers expect that continuous training will be the norm (according to Pew Research, 61 percent of Americans under the age of 30 figure they will have to acquire new skills at some point in their careers).[142] Companies continuously need workers with evolving skills, and surely the best people to acquire those skills would be those they've already vetted and employed. It makes perfect sense, right? Except that it's never really worked that way.

North American companies have always been reticent about training. Why spend too much on it, goes the rationale, when that worker can use it to get another job at another company? To be sure, there is something to be said for that view. In December 2017, a time when the U.S. labor market was in full swing and companies were hiring at a nice clip, 3.25 million Americans quit their jobs, a number that had not been seen since the dot-com bubble was buoying the economy 16 years earlier.[143] So yes, it appears that when times are good, people are okay with ditching the job and company they have and looking for better prospects.

As a result, the training figures speak for themselves: in 2014, U.S. companies spent $55.4 billion on training—less than the $55.5 billion they'd spent eight years earlier, in 2006. This should not, however, be a big surprise. North American companies like poaching—sometimes couched as "finding new talent"—much better than they like training. The poaching mindset certainly dominated during the recession and the tough years that followed. The rationale went something like this: "We've got no time to train or invest, so we have to focus on parachuting in the perfect person."

In the summer of 2016, I saw that attitude firsthand while I was doing some research on the technology sector in Canada. I spoke to many in the "tech hub" of Ontario's Kitchener-Waterloo area, some of whom were desperate to get government clearance to bring in what they considered perfect-fit workers from Silicon Valley. Why not train, I asked? The answer was inevitably that training was not a practical solution. The world was moving too quickly, and they had no time create the expertise they needed. "If we can't get the workers we want, we may have to just move the whole operation down to California so we can staff up the way we need to," one manager told me.

That "poach 'em if you need 'em" attitude may still prevail when it comes to the most elite workers, but there is evidence that companies are beginning to think harder about training from within, or at least about developing the people they have. That learning and development (L&D) spending that plunged for eight years in the United States has since shot up, to the point where companies were spending $93.6 billion on it in 2017. It's a huge difference, an increase of almost 70 percent since 2014. Of course, the recession had a lot to do with that; L&D budgets, like all budgets, were under the gun for years.[144] But there's more to it. The fact is that, at this point in time, companies that invest in training are giving themselves a huge advantage over those that do not.

Once again, tech companies are on the leading edge of this trend, and coming up with some creative approaches. In 2018, Google announced that it was turning its internal IT training program into an online course, and that it would be offering 10,000 scholarships for students to use it, no strings attached. Although Google clearly hoped to hire from within that pool of new graduates, it also accepted that many—perhaps the majority—of those whose education it funded would *not* end up working there, and it was cool with that. In short, it accepted that it was training the workforce its industry needed, and trusted that this was something that would work for everyone over the long term.[145] This type of approach represents a sharp about-face from the mentality that has prevailed in North America for so long, and perhaps marks a turning point for the economy as a whole.

For companies looking for inspiration, the poster child for how to reboot an entire company from within is AT&T. Once upon a time, the corporation was a utility—it was *the* phone company in the U.S. Following deregulation in the 1980s and '90s, and a massive shakeup in the telecommunications industry, it became a combination of a media company and a telecom business—and continues to evolve all the time. The technology the company employs now is different from what it used a couple of decades ago. Despite the massive changes, some employees have stuck with the firm the entire time. That this has been allowed to happen, and to actually work well, has a lot to do with a decision the company made a decade ago to aggressively retrain and continuously train the staff it has, rather than simply move them along and start anew. The decision was pragmatic. As one executive put it, AT&T came to the realization that "we could go out and try to hire all these software and engineering people and probably pay through the nose to get them but even that wouldn't have been adequate . . . or we could try to reskill our existing workforce so they could be competent in the technology and the skills required to run the business going forward."[146]

It has not been an inexpensive initiative: the company's plan for "reskilling" (known internally as FutureReady) has cost approximately $1 billion and includes everything from online courses to the creation of a career center that allows employees to figure out what jobs they would like to train for and how much demand the company will have for them in the future. As detailed in a case study published in the *Harvard Business Review* in 2016, about 140,000 employees are involved in the program, and the expectation is that they will change roles every four years.[147]

As the talent crunch deepens, the type of thinking exhibited by Google and AT&T makes more and more sense in terms of the firms' self-interest. Creating a more highly skilled workforce or retraining your existing employees are both smart bets. However, there is potentially a broader role for business in the work world of the future—a leadership role that relates to health of the economy as a whole. The Googles and AT&Ts may be trailblazers, but they are focusing on a fairly narrow slice of the labor-force pie. Stories of businesses choosing to train unskilled or lower-skilled workers are much harder to come by. For sure, there are a few—such as the ones in Vermont and Quebec that we looked at in chapter 2, which are so demographically pressed that they feel they have no other option. Generally speaking, however, retraining for those whose jobs are disappearing, due to automation or otherwise, tends to be left to governments, or sometimes to trade unions in partnership with business. Perhaps that needs to change. Maybe business needs to take a more active role in training, becoming an active partner in what is going to be a significant shift for the both the economy and the labor force.

The alternative, of course, is simply to lay off workers, and that is going to be an inevitable part of the story for the next decade. It will not happen immediately: as we've seen, demographics are protecting workers right now, and in most industries, automation is not the threat it may eventually be to lower-skilled workers. But we've talked about truck drivers, who are now in short supply, and about Uber and taxi drivers, who are caught in an ongoing battle. If self-driving vehicles do become a reality (and there is a plausible case to be made that they will, even if it takes a decade or more), *all* of these job categories will disappear. That's different from getting the job done in a different way (as happened when secretaries started to type on word processors rather typewriters), and different from having some jobs disappear slowly as work functions change (when secretaries stopped being hired because most professionals were doing their own typing on personal computers and sending emails rather than letters). To be sure, there is a huge role for government in all of the displacement ahead, but there is a clear role for business, too, and it is one worth considering sooner rather than later.

HURRAY FOR HOLLYWOOD

It's about the talent. It's about the talent. It's about the talent. Those who work in Hollywood are familiar with this mantra, but the time has come for it to spread beyond La-La Land and into organizations across all industries. In a world where the focus needs to be on the end product, the point is not to fully staff a traditional workforce, but rather to plug in talent where it needs to be in order to get the job done. And so, we're back to the point we've been discussing all along: we are, in many ways, in a post-jobs world—and that is just fine. Succeeding in this new world could mean engaging with freelancers and bringing people in on a part-time or contract basis, or as consultants. It may also mean thinking of workers not as workers, per se, but as talent, and doing whatever it takes to engage them in the project at hand, whether a short-term endeavor or a plan that will take a decade to complete.

This could mean accommodating workers in whatever way is necessary. Does your company have older workers who might need better lighting over their workstations, or a flexible schedule? That could be part of the solution. What about better parental leaves or other accommodations for parents, or for those dealing with aging relatives? Add it to the list. Even telecommuting (which we'll explore in greater detail in chapter 7) should be part of the discussion, whether employers like it or not (they do not). This type of focus on employee wellbeing isn't exactly new; rather, it represents a continuation of discussions that have been brought up for decades, and then put on hold when the economy lost steam.

Picking up the thread of those discussions, and hanging on to it regardless of economic conditions, will require that companies shift their mindset. But perhaps the most important thing they can do to get the employees they want is to stop thinking about getting employees at all and instead focus on getting the work done. Those employees who are most in demand will have options—for instance, whether to seek work as an employee or a contingent worker—and increasingly, many will decide that the gig route works best for them. It is interesting that in the 2001 book *The War for Talent* (which was excerpted in the *Harvard Business Review*), an example of someone—not some company—with a good talent mindset was director Steven Spielberg, who at the time was working on the first *Jurassic Park* movie. Directors like Spielberg do not employ people for long; they bring them in for a time to work on a project and then release them. That Hollywood model of work may well be the future for North America, even if it requires a leap of faith for both companies and individuals.

CHAPTER 7

MANAGING THE MAZE

My audience was gasping; some members actually looked a little terrified. The reason? I was detailing the way that one company I knew of forced its employees to take vacations—and then forced them *not* to check their email while away. It was a radical, insane concept: I might as well have been describing a sci-fi fantasy in which the world is overtaken by giant beetles or something. They laughed nervously and nudged each other, whispering about just how well that idea would go over where *they* worked.

I was speaking to a group of accountants and finance professionals in Phoenix, Arizona, and they clearly were used to a more conventional workplace model, one in which people were not forced to take vacations, and when they did book a few days away, were apt (and even expected) to check in with their office. In fact, when the organizer thanked me for speaking about the trends reshaping the economy, he joked that their industry was not endorsing anything as radical as the scenario I'd just presented.

Fair enough. Not every model of work will work for every organization. There are many different models for the workplace, and a one-size-fits-all approach is a poor one to take, now more than ever. The workplace of the future is going to be complicated, and will likely include a bit of everything: organizations where everyone works together in the office; others where employees meet only for special occasions; and still others where everyone is a contractor. Not to mention, of course, countless combinations of all of the above. No doubt some will also include workers who swoop in to complete the task at hand and then take vacations without looking back.

If companies are going to be productive and compete effectively in a challenging marketplace, they have to craft the right model of work for their organization and figure out how to manage competing priorities. Once upon a time, the landscape was fairly homogenous: you had one main model of how a workplace was structured, and that meant one set of concerns for managers and human resources departments. Now, as we've seen, there are many different models for organizing work and determining who to employ—and that means a whole new set of things with which organizations will have to contend. Do you actually have to train contractors, or just invite them to the holiday party and call it good? How do you handle security when people are coming and going in different roles? Should you embrace the work-at-home culture, or avoid it like the plague? In the years to come, companies will be grappling with a whole new set of questions and possibilities—some, perhaps, as radical as enforced downtime.

But hey, why not? The reality is that the work world is changing. Technology, demographics, new models—all are in play, so why pretend this isn't the case? Imposing the same old rules on what is a completely new structure just because that's the way things have always been done makes little sense. Perhaps it's time to finally experiment with different models of work—and different models of time off as well. It may not be easy to navigate the maze of options, but make no mistake: paths through the maze do exist.

BUILDING A TEMPORARY TEAM

The rise of the gig economy—and with it, other forms of nontraditional work—is going to shake things up in companies big and small. We talked about the gig economy in chapter 4, but most of that discussion, as tends to be the case on this topic, took the workers' point of view. Integrating nontraditional workers into companies is another thing entirely, with a whole different set of considerations. From a management perspective, it perhaps makes sense to frame things in a way that might be more appealing, or at least easier to wrap one's head around: it's not so much that you'll be bringing nontraditional workers into the fold, but that you'll be embracing that tried-and-true "Hollywood Model" we've discussed elsewhere.

To recap: films are generally made using a team of workers who show up, complete the project, and then move on. Sure, there is always a core group of studio-employed workers who make decisions on projects and then deal with administration and finance. Everyone else, though, is parachuted in on a temporary basis. Those coordinating the project have to spend their time finding the right people, bringing them together, and then managing them for the duration. Actors are, of course, at the top of the list of those who must be assembled, but the system is the same for camera operators and makeup artists and production assistants: the best talent is found, with the expectation that they will be there for a time, be well compensated for their work, and then move on. This is not a model that's been prevalent in the corporate world, but perhaps its time is coming.

Of course, the talent that comes together on a film set does not come together randomly, which is something those in the corporate world should note. Those who group and regroup on film sets know who they like to work with, and they do their best to assemble those folks time and time again. Director Tim Burton has worked with actor Johnny Depp eight times, on a series of weird and dark films for which they both apparently have an affinity. Actor Tom Hanks hired makeup artist Dan Striepeke for 17 films, moving on to someone else only when Striepeke retired. Teams, loosely or rigidly organized, tend to reassemble again and again for projects.

The era we are entering in the business world will certainly have Hollywood-type teams, although how many of those team members are giggers and how many are permanent will vary. In some cases, teams may be composed of mostly permanent employees, with one or two "extras" parachuted in, perhaps as team leaders. The proliferation of gig executives we're seeing (as discussed in chapter 6) suggests that this model may become quite popular. It works on many levels: on a cost basis, it can be quicker and cheaper to bring in someone this way, and it can also allow a company to access needed skills on a specific project. But regardless of whether we're talking about executive-level help or workers with less seniority, companies that want to use contract staff effectively will have to work harder at it than they may have had to do in the past.

Followed incorrectly, the freelancer route can more expensive than it might seem. On the surface, employees may be a lot more expensive than are freelancers, but if they stick around for a period of time, they become part of the "team," and investing in them gets you more than you pay for. With improperly managed freelancers, you get exactly what you pay for—which is to say that the work gets done, but there's no commitment to anything more. To be most effective on this front, companies need to think of the workers who are not directly in front of them as part of their "team," too, as a kind of virtual workforce that can be assembled quickly when needed. Of course, that may not always be possible: sometimes the freelancers who have been used in the past are not going to be available, perhaps because they are working on other assignments. But there are things companies can do to ensure that freelancers look favorably upon them when it comes time to decide which job to take on.

Part of that equation might be to actually invest in non-permanent workers. It could start with something as simple as talking to them about the company's larger goals and where the work they do, however short-term, fits into the wider picture. In human resources parlance, that's called "onboarding"—a.k.a., orienting people to a company in a positive way. But what happens when it's time for that employee to leave? At that end of the bargain, companies can devise an exit strategy, one that leaves the door open for the best of these workers to come back as needed. In a broader sense, companies may just have to be "nicer" to contractors. Some have referred to this need as the creation of an "arm's-length embrace,"[148] in which companies strive to establish an ongoing relationship with contingent workers.

Actually, whether their contingent workers are on- or offsite at a given time, companies should give some thought to how they treat them. Those who doubt that piece of advice would do well to consider a study by the global consulting firm Willis Towers Watson released in May 2018. After polling more than 100,000 workers across 112 companies, the consulting firm found that contingent workers generally reported a positive work experience, and that in terms of performance, they tended to score higher than did other workers. That said, in several areas they felt more challenged than those who were actually employees. Most notably, many cited what they saw as an unfair amount of work as a negative, as was a misalignment about company goals and poor decision speed.[149] "It's a bit of a detract from the lonely worker hypotheses," says Tracey Malcolm, the Global Future of Work Leader at Willis Towers Watson, noting that contingent workers are generally happy with the companies they work for. Still, she adds, "It is also a support to the point—if nuanced—that contingents can suffer from feeling 'overloaded' with work others on the 'team' may not be getting, and their need to feel connected to the purpose and decisions going on in the organization."

It may seem like a radical concept, but companies should also give some thought to training their gig workers. In chapter 6, we talked about how the training of workers in general nosedives as soon as there is a need to cut costs, but it still bears consideration. In an era when Google has decided to train people who may never end up working for it as a way to build a better overall workforce, perhaps the time has come for companies to invest in workers they might use on a temporary but ongoing basis. It's worth noting, however, that this is a fraught topic from a legal perspective, in that companies who provide training are often thought to have crossed a line and created "employees." Perhaps that needs to be addressed by a change in legislation: the old rules really apply to an old model of work. In the meantime, companies may need to confer with their legal departments to make sure that they are on the right side of existing rules.

Companies that think any or all of this seems unnecessary for workers who are just commodities of a sort should remind themselves that we are living in a world of instant online reviews. We've all looked at Yelp before checking out a new restaurant, or consulted TripAdvisor before booking a hotel room. Would-be workers are no different. Before accepting assignments, freelancers are going to check out company reviews on sites like GlassDoor or Indeed—and those who are in demand may be more likely than the average to do so. If plenty of companies want freelance talent, and are paying similar rates, what's going to make one stand out to a prospective worker? It may well be the experience of those who have already worked there, an experience that will be reflected in their reviews. Similarly, one simple way an employer can create goodwill with standout nontraditional workers is to provide positive reviews for their website or LinkedIn profiles.

Goodwill can be created in other ways. One manager, writing for the *Entrepreneur* magazine website, noted that when he posts a job ad online, he makes a point of acknowledging everyone who applies, even if he's not interested in hiring them. "You wouldn't believe the effusive thank yous I get for these simple rejection emails because it is such a departure from how freelancers are treated," he writes. He adds that when he has gone back to people later on, the conversation goes much more smoothly because he has a "respectful foundation" from which to build.[150]

In *The Culture Code*, author Daniel Coy writes about the usefulness of "belonging cues," or signs that people are connected to someone who cares about them. He argues that when organizations make an effort on this front, workers frequently perform better, and he cites several examples to prove the point. In one of the most illustrative, he highlights a study of 772 Australian patients who were admitted to hospital after attempting suicide. After their release, half of the former patients received a personalized postcard asking how they were doing and ending with "If you wish to drop us a note, we would be happy to hear from you." Over the following two years, those patients who received the postcards were half as likely to be readmitted. Lesson: a small signal can have a big effect.[151]

And so it may be with gig workers. Perhaps no one's life is on the line, but reaching out with the occasional email or note to the "virtual workforce" can make a big difference when the time comes to reassemble a team. And it's possible to go further. I sometimes ask audiences of managers and HR executives if they include gig workers on the list of holiday party invitations. If the answer is yes, it's generally because those people are on contract at the time of the party, and even then, not everyone is included. Almost no one thinks to invite those who worked for them earlier in the year. Of course, the invitation is not mandatory (and goodness knows many people dread the annual party anyway). Reaching out, however, *is* something to think about, given that it may lead to a better response rate over the coming year.

Another approach to temporary team building is to think beyond cocktails (or even a full sit-down dinner) and offer something really substantial: benefits. That's right, maybe contractors should get benefits from their temporary employers, or at least have access to them. It is slowly happening, at least at some levels. In 2017, for example, Willis Towers Watson announced a strategic alliance with Stride Health, a benefits provider for independent workers, with the idea of providing access to benefits for contingent workers such as contractors, part-timers, and seasonal talent. Companies like Stride allow workers to pay for benefits themselves (or have them paid for by their employers for the time that they are working at a company), taking them with them as they move from employer to employer. This model, or some form of "portable benefits," could be a game-changer for those who want to go the gig route, and for the companies who want to hire them.

EMBRACING THE TELECOMMUTE

Want a way to work with your colleagues without actually being in the same office? You could turn to Google for some cool technology. From Google handouts to Google docs, the company's offerings are all about collaboration without having to be in the same place at the same time. Want to get a job that allows you to work in a different place than your colleagues? Well . . . don't work at Google. Turns out they expect you to show up at the office every day; no remote work allowed.

Actually, it's not fair to pick on Google; it's hardly alone in wanting all of its workers together in actual company space. Although statistics show that telecommuting is on the rise in North America, many high-profile companies—including IBM, the company that really started the trend many years ago with the notion of the "anytime, anywhere workforce"—have been retreating from previously articulated plans that allow it. Whether organizations are worrying about workers logging hours on their March Madness picks rather than their actual work (because that never happens when people are physically at the office, right?) or concerned about security breaches (fair enough), the upshot is the same: telecommuting is kind of yesterday's man when it comes to human resources practices. For the sake of productivity, though, we can only hope that the pendulum swings the other way, and that we once again start encouraging work from home, or from wherever. Because once employers do accept that work is not a place, the world will open up for them in terms of the labor pool—and that's not an insignificant consideration at a time when the talent crunch is reaching a peak.

To be sure, not everyone's job can be done offsite. A hairstylist needs to be in the salon, and a nurse needs to be in the hospital or other care institution. For many jobs, however, some work can indeed be done remotely—and it turns out there's a high correlation between the ability to work offsite and advanced education. According to a report from Flexijobs and Global Workplace Analytics, 53 percent of U.S. remote workers have at least a bachelor's degree, as compared with 37 percent of those who do not telecommute.[152]

The numbers show that a healthy chunk of North America's workforce does work remotely, at least some of the time. A 2016 survey by the Society of Human Resource Managers found that in the 20 years since 1996, the percentage of organizations offering some form of telecommuting tripled from 20 percent to 60 percent,[153] while a Gallup poll found that, as of 2016, 43 percent of U.S. workers were able to work remotely at least some of the time, and that 75 percent did so more than one-fifth of the time.[154] Comparable Canadian figures are not readily available (the latest Statistics Canada figures are based on the 2016 census, and found that 7.4 percent of Canadians worked from home), but the anecdotal evidence is clear in both countries: working from somewhere other than the office is a growing trend, and it succeeds in a number of levels.

From a societal point of view, telecommuting makes sense. If more people did it, individual stress levels and health outcomes would arguably win big. As of 2016, the average worker in the United States commuted for 26.6 minutes a day, while the average Canadian spent 26.2 minutes. In both countries, people tended to use their own vehicles, with only 5.4 percent of U.S. commuters and 12.4 percent of their Canadian counterparts choosing public transit.[155] None of this is particularly good for the environment, or a good use of people's time (particularly in and near cities, where commute times can be much longer and more stressful). One study of commuters done in the U.K. found that 55 percent were stressed by their commute; as well, workers whose time was gobbled up by commuting tended to eat worse and lead less active and healthy lifestyles than those who had more manageable commutes or did not commute at all. That report went as far as to suggest that employers allow flexible schedules and working from home as a way to improve national health.[156] Other studies also suggests that workers who telecommute tend to be less stressed than those who do not, with a 2014 study by software service provider PGi finding that 80 percent of remote workers had higher morale than those who worked at the office; 82 percent said it helped to lower their stress levels.[157]

Certainly, the environment would benefit if more people worked from home. Calculations by Global Workplace Analytics suggest that if 40 percent of the workforce in the United States worked at home half of the time (based on half of the workforce being able to, and 80 percent wanting to), we could reduce greenhouse gases by 54 million tons, reduce wear and tear on the highways by over 119 billion miles a year (a big consideration, given the strain on public funding earmarked for road repair), and save more than 640 million barrels of oil. Oh, and prevent almost 90,000 traffic-related injuries or deaths to boot.[158]

Encouraging telecommuting could even help cool off the crazy-hot real estate markets in many North American cities. Over the past decade, and particularly since the recession, cities have been the prime centers of job growth in the United States and Canada. As a result, they have disproportionately attracted population and created a sharp demand for housing, which has been accompanied by a subsequent rise in home prices. From New York to Vancouver to Atlanta to Toronto, tales of woe abound. It's incredibly difficult—and incredibly expensive—for workers to get a toehold in the housing market, but living anywhere else is impossible, since cities are where the jobs are. Tech-fueled San Francisco is perhaps the most extreme example of this scenario: the average home price is $1.6 million, and a minimum income of $333,270 is required to afford one. The result, as we saw in chapter 5, is that there are reportedly more dogs in the city than children.[159] In Canada, a 2018 study by real estate company Royal LePage looked at the situation for "peak millennials" (those born between 1987 and 1993) and suggested that they were finding affordability a challenge. "For peak millennials, the group which makes up the bulk of our first-time homebuyers, the path to property ownership has been a challenging one," Royal LePage president and CEO Phil Soper was quoted as saying. "In our largest cities, it is difficult for young people to purchase a home on a single household income."[160]

If remote work were encouraged, the pressure on home prices would certainly lessen in city cores, and might even out a bit through the metropolitan areas around cities. But what about suburbs and exurbs that are farther out, or even towns that are not in the immediate vicinity? They, too, stand to gain. The aging of the population in North America is happening much more quickly in non-urban areas, as younger people leave to find work in the cities. As a result, there is a very uneven split between the housing markets within and outside of cities, and certain places in Canada and the United States have very affordable housing that's eliciting limited interest from younger households. If workers could live and work from anywhere, whole regions could be revitalized. This ability to earn a city wage while living in a completely different—and lower-cost—area is sometimes called "wage arbitrage." It is happening, albeit slowly. If it is going to grow more substantially, concentrated efforts will need to be made. Vermont is doing just that. In 2018, taking into account the state's rapidly aging population, the government offered cash payments to those who move there and decide to telecommute.[161]

Of course, telecommuting isn't all sunshine and rainbows. As we saw earlier, loneliness is a real issue. And there's the basic fact that some people want to work from home and some do not. "I like to get dressed up and have somewhere to go every day," said a business columnist when I asked her if she ever choses to work from home. Fair enough: her home wasn't too far from the newspaper where she worked, and her children were grown, meaning they didn't need her to rush home and shuttle them somewhere. Her circumstances meant that commuting to an office was A-OK with her. Many millennial workers, however, think differently. A 2014 survey by the Conference Board of Canada found that more than 70 percent would prefer to telecommute than physically go to an office.[162]

But never mind the environment or loneliness or anything else: Does telecommuting make sense for companies? The fact that so many are pulling away from the practice suggests that it does not, yet legions of studies show that worker productivity rises when telecommuting is allowed. An excellent example comes from research by Stanford University professor Nicholas Bloom, who along with some colleagues studied workers at China's largest travel agency, Ctrip. The company's headquarters are in Shanghai, an expensive city by anyone's standards. In an effort to cut down on the office space it needs to lease, the company recruited volunteers to work from home four out of five days a week, The result? A 13 percent increase in productivity from those who worked remotely.[163] It's not so hard to see how this could come to pass. There are a lot of reasons why workers could be more productive away from the office than in it—from workplace distractions to the increased chance of catching the latest cold that's making the rounds (carried by sneezing co-workers who drag themselves in even when sick). But there are still challenges inherent in the practice.

Yahoo! is perhaps the most famous example of a high-profile organization that tried and then rejected telecommuting. The company had built a workforce around the idea that coming to work (and living in a hideously expensive area of California) was not strictly necessary, and for years it allowed employees to work from home. Then, in 2013, CEO Marissa Mayer ordered everyone back to work with a now-infamous memo sent by one of her human resources executives, explaining: "we need to be one Yahoo! and that starts with physically being together."[164] More recently, companies such as IBM and Best Buy have pulled back from allowing telecommuting, citing similar reasons.

Of course, not all companies agree. In the wake of the Yahoo! decision, Sir Richard Branson of the Virgin Group called the decision "old-school thinking,"[165] and Virgin remains a huge supporter of remote work. And in the years since Yahoo! threw in the towel on telecommuting, a consensus has yet to be reached as to whether it was a good or bad move. Nevertheless, it would seem that a majority of companies do think it will proliferate in the future, with a survey of business owners conducted by Virgin Media Business finding that they expect 60 percent of office-based employees to be working from home by 2022. Another survey by Office Angels, this time of employees, found that one-third expected commuting to be unheard of by 2036.[166]

To be sure, those companies that do go the telecommuting route will face challenges. A worker who is not on site is, in many ways, harder to manage and evaluate. This might mean that companies have to come up with new metrics, and find ways to effectively judge the output of workers who are not in the office day to day. Security, too, is a major issue. Following a series of high-profile data breaches (Yahoo!, Ebay, and Equifax come to mind), there is now a wide-ranging and ongoing conversation around the topic of security. Part of that discussion centers around the "Bring Your Own Device" (BYOD) issue, a growing trend that is popular with employees who find it easier to use their own technology to remotely access company networks than to rely on company-supplied tech. Not surprisingly, the practice has opened a slew of security and insurance issues, all of which will need to be sorted out.

But is it really—or only—security and evaluation issues that are driving companies to ban telecommuting? Or is something more at play? Could it be that some are moving away from the practice because they are eager to have their employees interact, rather than work in silos? It's a valid concern: bringing workers together and allowing them to interact sometimes results in more than the sum of the parts. If remote working is going to be successful going forward, companies will have to find a way to create that interaction, even when workers are not physically together all of the time.

RECREATING THE WATER COOLER (AND CREATING A CORPORATE CULTURE)

The water cooler. The office kitchen. The Starbucks outside the main doors where everyone grabs their three o'clock latte. All are potential time wasters, for sure. When co-workers gather, they are apt to discuss the latest episode of *Dancing with the Stars* or, if they're more work-focused, their dissatisfaction with their bonuses—and maybe not within a 10-minute window either. It's no wonder that managers look at their staff slacking off in any or all of these spots and think longingly about replacing the whole bunch with a nice, antisocial robot or two.

But here's the thing: the water cooler may have its downsides, but it has upsides too. Although you can certainly order all of your employees to stay stapled to their desks, the reality is that sometimes those *Dancing with the Stars* conversations lead to other things. As numerous studies have concluded, at the very least, those interactions offer a chance for co-workers to start to feel like a team and, by extension, to share information that could be helpful to their teammates.

That point was borne out by a 2009 Massachusetts Institute of Technology study. Using specially designed badges to track and record information—including the wearers' location, direction, and voice inflections—researchers tracked how and where workers interacted. The idea was to figure out how much time users were spending being social, and then look at how that correlated with their productivity. The results were telling. In one experiment that took place in a call center, the researchers found that cohesion (defined as how connected people were) around what they called a "tribe" was one of the largest factors in both productivity and job satisfaction. In another, they monitored IT workers and found once again that group cohesion was a central predictor of productivity, so much so that workers whose group cohesion was in the top third showed an increase in work productivity of more than 10 percent.[167]

So, there is something to be said for that water cooler effect—but how do you recreate it if everyone is telecommuting or spends a substantial amount of time away from their co-workers? Simple, some might say: just don't let them telecommute. But perhaps this isn't the only viable answer. Technology can go a long way toward creating a water cooler of sorts. Virtual meetings, for example, can be very effective in bringing teams together, whether via Skype or FaceTime or Google Hangouts.

Japan, which is desperately trying to contend with its aging population and lack of workers, is ahead of North America when it comes to technologies that can bring telecommuters into the office. One initiative is the use of robots called OriHime—sort of like nanny cams that give telecommuters a virtual presence in the office. Through the robots, remote workers are able to see exactly what is going on at the office all day, and their co-workers can even move the robots (which are about eight inches tall) from room to room, making it possible to take them to meetings in various conference rooms. Tokyo software company SonicGarden has taken a similar approach by setting up a "virtual office" that allows workers to see live feeds of each other on their computers.[168]

North American companies are also getting increasingly inventive when it comes to telecommuting. Amy Laski, who runs a virtual company called Felicity PR, has roughly 25 workers, all of whom do their jobs remotely. Despite the fact that her organization does not have a dedicated physical space, she considers her model very much that of a team, and she screens out those who are not good team players. Members are expected to continuously collaborate. "We do a lot of things to connect people," she told me when we spoke. "For example, we have something called the 'Team Water Cooler,' which is a private Facebook group that we are on all the time. We have an internal newsletter and professional development opportunities. And once a year, we do an all-day urban retreat where everyone gets together in a great ambiance with great food and great speakers." Felicity also has a downright retro policy called "Just Call," which is exactly what it sounds like. "It can take five emails trying to get in touch with someone just to set up a time to talk on the phone, when the matter can be quickly discussed—and resolved—in a two-minute phone conversation," she says. "Our policy is to 'Just call!' We want to make sure people are talking all the time."

SimpliFlying, an airline marketing-strategy company, is all about telecommuting. Its team, in the words of CEO Shashank Nigam, "can work from anywhere in the world, whenever they like. There are no fixed working hours. As long as deadlines are met. It's hard work, really. We have recently completed a project for a major aviation client in four weeks, which would have taken a traditional firm a year."[169] But despite the "work on your own" culture, SimpliFlying still brings its workers together throughout the year to enforce the corporate culture and to remind them that they are in fact a team. Meetings take place in destinations such as Las Vegas; Budapest, Hungary; and Colombo, Sri Lanka: it's hard to pick a central gathering spot when the team has members based in Singapore, India, Spain, Canada, and the U.K.

Encore.org, a nonprofit that fosters innovation around longer lives, social change, and intergenerational opportunities, tries to bring that innovation to bear within its own working culture. As vice president of strategic communications Marci Alboher put it when we spoke, "We try to walk the walk." Quite literally, in some cases: the company encourages workers to get out and walk with their colleagues. In New York–based Alboher's case, that means scheduling a "walk" with a Washington-based colleague every Monday at 7:30 a.m. Each on their own phone, and in their own city, they debrief each other on the weekend, get some exercise, and tee up their respective agendas for the work week. "Sometimes we follow up with emails right after," says Alboher, "but this is a great way to get things done." Like Felicity, Encore also looks for "old-fashioned" ways to bring employees together, even though cutting-edge technology is often employed to do so. "One of our employees had a baby last year, and we threw a virtual baby shower for him and his wife," she explains. "He works by himself in Oregon, but we were all together across the country on screens. He had a present we had sent, which he opened, and we all went around and showed baby pictures of ourselves, and it just felt like a party for an hour."

Of course, throwing a baby shower is not a guaranteed way to motivate workers— telecommuters or otherwise. However, creating a corporate culture and engaging workers with it is a proven technique. That may seem like an added challenge in a world where getting the right talent is already tough, but it can pay dividends, both in terms of attracting that talent in the first place, and then getting the most out of them.

EVERY DAY IS A VACATION

Telecommuting makes businesses uncomfortable enough, with workers here, there, and everywhere, and often hard to monitor. What to make, then, of policies that let people come and go at will, taking as much vacation time as they see fit? Apparently, we've entered this brave new world, though perhaps it's no surprise. For those who freelance or work virtually, the concepts of work and leisure are already blended: they sometimes work at night or on weekends or from the beach, and they can choose to do non-work-related tasks when they feel like it. (As one freelancer puts it, "Why would I choose to go to Costco on a Saturday, when there are tons of people, when I can go instead on a Tuesday morning and get in and out in a hurry? Efficiency-wise, it makes more sense to change it up.") Companies that want to attract talent should consider rethinking the traditional model of "time on" and "time off."

Some companies are already there. Netflix famously stopped tracking vacation time in 2004, accepting that its employees were putting in huge amounts of time on weekends and after traditional hours during the week. Virgin followed Netflix, imposing a similar plan for at least part of its business, and some small tech startups are also following suit. In almost all cases, the companies cited a need to attract the best talent as the reason behind the decision, although critics point to other motivations as well. In many cases in North America, unused vacation time "accrues," and the employee gets it in a lump—either as time or the paid equivalent—when they leave the company or retire. With unlimited-vacation plans, companies are not on the hook in this way, which can potentially save significant amounts of money. Others point out that, under "unlimited" policies, some workers could actually feel pressured into taking *less* vacation than they would have otherwise, since time off still must be approved by supervisors and employees might not want to be seen as abusing the policy.

Kronos, a company that makes workforce software, adopted an unlimited vacation policy in 2016 in response to difficulties in finding the talent they wanted. In a 2017 piece for the *Harvard Business Review*, CEO Aron Ain detailed the company's experiences. While he deemed it a success on many fronts, he admitted that implementation was not without its challenges. "I wasn't prepared for how much emotion and pushback this change would evoke, even for a small number of people," he writes. To be sure, a number of people within the company—he estimates 5 percent of the total—were unhappy. These were primarily managers who worried that the policy made their work harder, but there were also employees who liked the idea of not using their vacations and instead saving the accrued vacation pay as a kind of piggy bank for retirement. There were also veterans who thought it unfair, given that they'd put in years to "earn" the vacation time they'd been granted and believed others should have to serve their time as well.[170]

Realizing that granting vacation time may not necessarily translate into employees *taking* vacation time, some companies have gone one step further. Remember those frightened accountants in Phoenix I told you about at the beginning of this chapter? SimpliFlying was the company whose policies had them shaking in their boots. It requires that employees take a week off after each seven weeks they work, and that they do, in fact, make it a vacation. The policy mandates that no one check their email while away, and those who do have their pay docked. Writing about the experiment after its implementation phase, Nigam was enthusiastic: "The results have been nothing short of spectacular. Individual productivity levels shoot up in the weeks following the break for any one of us, creativity improves along with teamwork, and each of us is happier when we get back to work."[171]

For employers, this is a quantum leap, and it's not clear that many outside of the tech space will get there particularly quickly. North American businesses still value "face time," or "presenteeism," as it's sometimes called. Loosely translated, it means just showing up. Some companies take the concept further, into the realm of "competitive overtime." According to a study by the British procurement consulting firm Xoomworks, almost one-third (31 percent) of 1,000 office workers surveyed said they sent emails outside of work hours just to signal to others that they were working, while a small but strategic 4 percent went as far as using email schedulers to send early-morning messages. A whopping 54 percent of workers admitted to staying later than their colleagues just to impress their superiors. We shouldn't be surprised. After all, this is the same mentality that has people dragging themselves into work when they are ill or working through lunch everyday because everyone else does. That might be fine if it led to more productive companies, but creating stress and anxiety seems just as likely to cause conflict and burnout without contributing much to the bottom line. Netflix, after all, has revenues growing at something like 40 percent a year, and is responsible for something like one-third of all internet traffic.[172]

TOWARD A MORE COMPLICATED FUTURE

It is a maze, for sure, one comprising different types of workers and work styles, and it is going to get increasingly convoluted as we move forward. Indeed, as the impacts of technology and demographics merge, managing the workforce will become ever more fraught.

What kind of job stress is going to manifest itself, for example, if robots are physically marched into offices and introduced as new cubicle mates? It's not so far-fetched: they are already performing some job functions, and apparently getting along well enough with their human colleagues (at Fetch Robotics, they are called "pets"[173]). A bigger robot rollout, however, could bring a whole new dimension to those "my co-worker is so annoying" stories.

And what about the implications of longer working lives? We know life expectancy is creeping up, but by and large, this is not something business has given much thought to. Some believe that a child born in an advanced economy today has a 50 percent chance of living to the age of 100.[174] A 40-year work life may be inadequate to fund that kind of retirement, so the workforce could get much, much older. How exactly will that play out?

Right now, the biggest challenge for business is to break away from the full-time-employees-at-the-office model and make it work, but there is more change ahead. In this brave new world, flexibility, creativity, and an open mind may be the "skills" that make work work—for businesses and labor.

CHAPTER 8

THE GOVERNMENT OUGHT TO DO SOMETHING (BUT WHAT, EXACTLY?)

Like any new mother, Jodie, a 38-year-old personal trainer, was excited about taking some time away from work to spend with her new baby. And as a Canadian, she was in a seemingly good position to do so. In Canada, employment insurance covers 15 weeks of benefits (which can start as early as 12 weeks before giving birth) at 55 percent of the claimant's salary. Following the maternity benefits, there are another 35 weeks of protected parental leave available at 55 percent of salary, or 61 weeks of leave at 33 percent. Those options can be taken by one parent, or shared by both. If Jodie were American, her situation would not have been as favorable: she'd be entitled to only 12 weeks of unpaid leave (though some employers do offer better plans).

As it happens, though, when it came to maternity benefits, Jodie was not particularly well off by either Canadian or American standards. In fact, although she runs a small gym and pays into employment insurance for her employees, she's entitled to no personal coverage under the program. As a small business owner, she's not entitled to employment insurance under *any* circumstances. If she were a freelancer, as many trainers are, moving from gym to gym, she wouldn't have qualified for any leave either. Gig workers are not considered employees; hence, no coverage. Jodie ultimately did take some leave, but it was supported by her husband's salary rather than any government programs.

Jodie is not alone. In most of the industrialized world, employment-related policies are all about protecting workers in traditional jobs. This stands to reason. After all, many of these policies were crafted decades ago, at a time when work was very much a place where one showed up five days a week over the course of many years. From employment insurance to maternity benefits to income support programs, many of our policies hail from this bygone era, one that almost seems quaint these days. It was an era of unions, of full-time work, of one income supporting a family, of job security. In short, it was nothing like today. And so we find ourselves with a complicated labor market and a simple social insurance system. Think about it: if you're employed full time, you get paid regularly; if you become unemployed, you're eligible for employment insurance. What happens, though, if you work two part-time jobs, or short-term contracts, or are self-employed? You're subject to substantial income volatility, but you have very little in the way of protection during your work life. And during retirement, you are even more at risk in terms of protecting your income.

There have always been people who were not well protected by conventional policies. Small business owners, whether dentists or plumbers, have always had to figure out their own benefits and deal with financial dry periods. Now, however, we have growing numbers of independent business owners (some of them rather involuntary), and others who are hopping from one part-time job or contract to another. The alarm has been raised: in their October 2017 assessment of the global economy, the International Monetary Fund stated that "the rise of part-time employment and temporary contracts challenges the current structure of social insurance systems—instituted in many advanced economies in the aftermath of the Great Depression and World War II—which may be better equipped to handle 'binary' employment status (people in the labor force are either employed full-time or unemployed)." The report concluded: "a broader rethinking of the nature of social insurance may be needed."[175]

Reforming social policies is only one challenge governments will face in the years ahead. Given the disruptions created by technology and platforms that allow employers to schedule shifts according to their needs, and not those of their workers, we now have what in many ways is a radically different world. With that in mind, should the goal be to push back the clock and recreate a more traditional economy? If not (and one could argue that this ship has long since sailed), where does that leave us? Is there an effective way to prepare the population for the robot-powered future? Do we need to consider higher payouts to those whose jobs have been displaced by automation? Will governments be able to bring in enough tax revenue to support social programs and infrastructure spending in a world without conventional jobs? And just what role should the government play in this brave new future anyway?

As is the case with individuals and businesses, the next few years will be a time of great change for governments. All options are on the table as we move toward defining a new role for our leaders. This role cannot and should not be determined in isolation: business needs to be a full partner in determining the right path, and employees and workers of all varieties need to buy in. It will be a complicated future, requiring complicated solutions, and all parties need to be involved.

TURNING BACK THE CLOCK

Let's be honest: if you're a regular taker of cabs, you're happy that ride-sharing services now exist. The experience of taking an Uber or a Lyft is generally just *nicer* than taking a cab. The cars are newer and cleaner, the drivers tend to be more pleasant, and it's a cinch to pay. These are generalities, of course: there are truly lovely cabs and truly lovely cabbies as well, but too often they are exceptions to the rule. The majority of those who have switched from hailing cabs to using ride-sharing services would be horrified at the thought of legislation being used to make their ride of choice go away. After all, the existence of Uber may have been brutal for the taxi industry, but so is the existence of Netflix for video stores. If Netflix had been banned or taxed to death, Blockbuster might still be on every corner, but it would make little sense to ban the use of what is really more effective way to distribute entertainment.

And yet, some do believe that the best way to deal with our quickly changing economy and labor market is for governments to simply "make it go away." How? By passing legislation that makes it impossible for new industries to displace old ones. It's not so far-fetched. There have been several government-sponsored attempts to give the taxi industry an advantage over ride-sharing companies (or at least not put them at a disadvantage), and cities including London, England, and Vancouver, British Columbia, have either banned or been slow to accept such services. In the same vein, there are ongoing attempts to impose legislation on room-sharing service Airbnb; justifications range from the fact that room-sharing can drive up local real estate prices to the fact that renting out extra space to earn a bit of extra cash is a business, plain and simple. At the end of the day, however, we're faced with an obvious truth: there is huge public demand for the Lyfts and Airbnbs of the world. They are no more likely to "just go away" than those kiosks used by the fast food industry, or the robots now replacing many functions previously performed by lawyers.

So, if we can't stop the economy from changing, what can we do? There's no question that the coming changes in the economy will bring income disruptions, which is why so many are agitating for a so-called miracle solution: the basic income—a concept that may be a lot less basic than it sounds.

THE COMPLICATED BASIC INCOME

"A world inhabited only by robots, their billionaire owners and a large and increasingly restive population is the plotline for countless dystopian fantasies, but it's a reality that appears to be drawing closer," wrote Robert Reich, secretary of labor under President Clinton, in the *New York Times*. Now a professor at the University of California, Berkeley, Reich was reviewing a book about the need for a basic income. And he agreed with the author that the time had come to throw in the towel on the idea that everyone could make money in the labor market as it currently exists and instead "give people money" (which was the title of the book he was reviewing).[176] Really?

The universal basic income (UBI) is having a moment. Fueled by the visions of those dystopian fantasies, the likes of Bill Gates, Mark Zuckerberg, and Elon Musk have suggested that it may be time to simply write off large sections of the population when it comes to work and, in turn, write them checks so that they can eke out an existence. On the surface, it seems like a simple idea, but a whole lot has to happen before we give up on the idea of everyone earning a living and instead find a way to pay them not to. Some suggest that the UBI might prove to be a better and more efficient way of providing income support services to those currently receiving other benefits, such as welfare payments. If so, it certainly needs a good look. Others argue that a UBI could help smooth out income volatility, which would otherwise continue to be nightmare (potentially) for those in nontraditional employment. Again, this deserves consideration. The idea, however, that a UBI is a good solution for everything that will ail an economy in which tech is creating havoc is a nonstarter, and the side effects mean we should proceed pretty slowly on implementing one.

Let's start by reiterating that the premise that all jobs are going to disappear is flat-out wrong. We know, for example, that companies are still going to need top-level executives and elite talent. We also know that there will be jobs, in one form or another, for those whose creativity cannot completely be overtaken by robots; for example, those in the caring professions, or anyone whose job requires high degrees of human contact. Even the most dire predictions of how many jobs will be replaced by robots do not suggest that they *all* will be.

Musk and his cohorts, you'll notice, don't seem ready to stop handing out their own big checks. On the contrary, they're building ever more luxurious offices and looking for creative ways to lure the workers they want. However, they also seem to have a somewhat guilty understanding of their own plans, which include automating every single function they can and doing away with as many bottom-line workers as possible. Not really a surprise, then, that they are leading the call for government to do something (read: hand out money) about the situation they themselves have created.

No one is arguing that workers as a whole will lose their edge as automation takes hold. We may not be looking at mass unemployment, per se— at least not in a hurry—but we will likely see periods of joblessness for many, as well as extreme income volatility. A worker who gets a job for a few months at an Amazon warehouse and then moves on to sporadic work at a seniors' home may never be classified as unemployed, but they will be constantly worrying about their job prospects and their income. They will be the new Uber drivers, inhabiting whatever replaces Uber as the place for those scrambling for a way to bring in some fast cash. It's not hard to construct a worst-case scenario from such a vision. With people living paycheck to paycheck (as is often the norm in North America), and not knowing when that next paycheck is coming, the implications are ugly.

Hence the appeal of a universal basic income. Defining it is actually harder than it would seem, but generally, it's akin to a "negative income tax," or a way to ensure that no one's income falls below a certain level. Although there are various ideas about how it will be implemented, the simplest model is the one in which everyone (that's the "universal" part) is sent a check for some amount of money—say, $1,000 a month. That actually seems kind of cool: after all, who couldn't use an extra $12,000 a year? One issue, though, is what it would be spent on. After all, if you're already employed and covering the basics, the idea of a "gifted" $12,000 a year is dazzling. A dream vacation to a Disney resort? Finally doing that kitchen reno (or part of it)? A check for $12,000 would be super-useful for all kinds of middle-class purposes, but presumably this is not the intent of such a program. In a much darker vein, some question the wisdom of distributing free money at a time when we're spending a lot of time and significant funds worrying about and treating an opioid epidemic. Under the circumstances, sending out a bunch of money every month to people, no strings attached, seems foolish.

Although this gets scant attention in discussions of UBI, there's also the issue of how inflationary it could be if you handed out checks across the board. That is, if everyone who calls a contractor about a reno has $12,000 in their pocket, the contractor will naturally raise his prices. So will Disney, if faced with ever-growing crowds. And so it will go, from groceries to real estate, to the point where the extra $1,000 a month will not buy what people had previously thought of as $1,000 worth of goods and services. Although proponents of the plan scoff at that concern, it's hard to argue that there would be no inflationary effects at all, or that they, in turn, wouldn't be addressed by policies such as higher interest rates from central banks.

At its worst, a UBI would act as a huge disincentive to trying to find work, something that would be particularly problematic if implemented at the same time that demographic trends were creating labor supply shortages. Consider what would happen if, for example, for every dollar you earned, you had to give back a dollar of your UBI (which is how many welfare programs work). You might not bother to look for work at all unless you were sure you could earn well in excess of the UBI. There are real fears that this could lead to a self-perpetuating cycle of people being out of the labor market and, for all intents and purposes, being encouraged to stay out of it.

All of that said, there are reasons why the UBI is an interesting idea. If we do end up in a place where many households are dealing with precarious employment and income insecurity, we will certainly need to create an array of social programs—of one form or another—to serve their needs. Perhaps a simple and straightforward UBI would be an elegant way of dealing with the issue.

The income volatility issue is only going to get worse, and perhaps some watered-down version of a UBI, taxed away for those who manage to earn more than it pays out, might not be a bad idea. That means decoupling the idea of a basic income from the idea of a "negative income tax" (basically guaranteeing a minimum income), and instead thinking of it as a smoothing mechanism, a sum of money that can be accessed in a month where income is low or nonexistent. This would be almost impossible to implement, though; if the UBI were indeed universal, it would be going to those who were not seeking any kind of paid work at all. Wages for stay-at-home parents, for example, are a whole other subject of debate and are not really something that needs to be addressed by a program meant to smooth wages for gig economy workers.

Another intriguing aspect of the UBI is that it would take us away from the "binary" policies mentioned earlier, where one is considered either employed or unemployed. At present, in order to qualify for any kind of assistance when your income slips, the reason for the slippage has to be that you lost your job; no gig workers need apply. The UBI could potentially be a way around that, acting as an income stabilizer to that large and growing group that is outside the realm of traditional employment. To be sure, this moves beyond the idea that a UBI is all about ensuring a minimum income, but it is worth contemplating. Finally, a UBI could also act as a way to restore some degree of power. Someone who is receiving $1,000 a month, for example, could decide not to grab the first (perhaps subpar) job that comes along out of sheer desperation. If this premise plays out across hundreds of thousands of workers, the thinking goes, employers would be forced to offer better pay and benefits than they might have otherwise. Of course, this could be wishful thinking: rather than paying workers more, the alternative for a fast food chain, for example, might just be to roll out the kiosks instead.

Even with all of those intriguing scenarios kicking around, there's something important to keep in mind. If governments go the UBI route, something would have to give to make up for the spending: by some estimates, the cost of a $1,000-a-month UBI program would be between 5 and 35 percent of GDP in most countries, which is not a cost that can be borne without slashing some existing programs.[177] Whether it's welfare payments or libraries or both, the choices are not likely to be popular.

* * *

So, what of the countries that have given the UBI a test run? Way back in the 1970s, Canada was one of the first countries to take a shot, in Dauphin, Manitoba. For five years, between 1974 and 1979, the most impoverished residents of the tiny prairie town were sent checks, with no strings attached, as part of a program nicknamed "Mincome." The federal and provincial governments shared the costs, and residents who applied and met the eligibility criteria were basically given 60 percent of what was deemed at the time to be the low-income cutoff for the area. Although a final report on the project was never released, there seems to be some consensus that it was effective in alleviating poverty, perhaps because individuals were free to work without having to give any of the money back.[178]

When it comes to more recent examples, Finland tops the pile—both because it tried such a bold experiment and because it unceremoniously abandoned it. Actually, the plan the country adopted in 2017 was not a true universal basic income, but a tweak to existing unemployment insurance programs in which a random sample of 2,000 unemployed people were given 560 euros a month (about US$656), no strings attached. They could look for work, or they could choose to live on the money, and even if they took a job, they would continue to get the money as a kind of bonus payment. It was a two-year project that was always intended to end in January 2019, which is exactly what the government decided to do. Critics say that the trial was too short and too limited to really yield any useful results.

Many other countries, including India, Japan, Iraq, South Africa, Belgium, Bulgaria, and the Czech Republic, have either experimented with basic incomes or are launching pilot projects, as are certain parts of the United States and Canada. While it is difficult to draw one sweeping conclusion from myriad projects with myriad rules, it does seem that, overall, many of these programs have been effective at raising people out of poverty. If we believe that the future we're heading for will hasten the spread of poverty, it may eventually be necessary to have a discussion about social welfare policies that eradicate it. At this point, though, particularly in North America, it makes much more sense to try to prevent that kind of future than accept it.

Of course, as alluded to above, the real problem with the UBI is that it would be freakishly expensive, and would have to be implemented at a time when government finances are already under pressure from both the unwinding of the basic employment model and an aging population. There are ways to make it work, of course, but none are especially appealing. One is simply to make the UBI not exactly universal, by taxing it away if you hit a certain income threshold, or to not give it out at all if you are at a certain income level. Regardless, it seems certain that a universal basic income could not be implemented without some kind of increased taxation on businesses, which would seem to ultimately have negative consequences for workers as well.

So, what are the alternatives to the UBI? One idea that has occasionally been proposed is a kind of enhanced socialist state where the government does not hand out money, per se, but where many other things are provided. For example, a proposal out of University College London's Institute for Global Prosperity (IGP) suggests that the model of socialized medicine prevalent in the U.K. (as well as in Canada and other countries) should be expanded to other areas, including the provision of homes, meals, transportation, internet access, and telephone service for those on low incomes, under a program it calls "Universal Basic Services." The reasoning is that such a program could be provided at less than the cost of a UBI, and that it may well be needed in a future in which technology has killed jobs.[179]

Maybe we need to brainstorm other ideas as well. We know, for example, that it is difficult even now for those without conventional jobs to borrow money, whether for car loans or mortgages or anything else (financial institutions truly seem to hate the gig economy!). Might there be a role for governments in helping nontraditional workers access credit markets? Perhaps not; if financial institutions see something as a bad risk, it seems like folly for governments to jump in and take it on. The reality, though, is that the conventional ways of doing things are crumbling, and the time has come to start a conversation about solutions, beyond the basic income, that will allow people to cope with the new future.

The UBI may work as an anti-poverty measure, and it may be a more effective way to deliver incomes to those truly in need than existing welfare programs. But as a Band-Aid solution to the issues created by a future in which work and work structures are being rethought, it is not likely to be nearly as effective as anyone would like. It's true that if we move to an age of driverless cars, then drivers will be out of work, but are we really willing to accept that they will have no future beyond collecting $12,000 a year from the government? That's not an acceptable vision of the future, and we shouldn't convince ourselves that it's the only possible outcome.

NEW POLICIES FOR A NEW WORLD

And so we have this new world emerging, with a lot of different pieces. Demographics are taking us one way and economics another, and every company and organization feels as if it's pressed to the wall. For every worker who accepts a job at a plant-filled, spa-inspired work space in Silicon Valley, there are many more who are dealing with a much more uncertain (and likely less pleasant) reality.

For government, there are competing priorities. The first is to create an environment in which people can be readied for the evolving labor market and the disruptions of automation, whether that means training, retraining, or coming up with other solutions. The next is to reform current policies in a way that will better serve a labor market that has changed since those policies were created. Last, and absolutely not least, governments need to prepare for the impact that all of this will have on their own bottom lines.

Worker Education, Training, and Retraining
Readying people, education-wise, for the next economy is a Herculean feat, one that means encouraging educational policies both for younger people coming up through the system and for existing workers looking to transition to new jobs when and if their skills become less in demand. This is one area in which the government can get to work—although legislating protections may not be the best approach. Efforts to change the human capital equation have the potential to allow workers to evolve with the market. Ideally, we would get to a point where workers whose jobs have been eliminated (by technology or otherwise) are nimble about getting to the next ones, and where portfolio careers and gig work may proliferate because workers like it that way and are perhaps using a series of gigs to get to their next career. The real role of government in such a world, then, may not be to change the future that is taking shape, but to craft policies that allow workers to best navigate it in its eventuality.

To start, a key goal could be to help the most vulnerable workers change their human capital characteristics so they are not vulnerable in the first place. We are a long way from the days when a high school education (or even less) would guarantee at least some kind of decent-paying factory or service-economy work. Many of those jobs are gone and not coming back, killed by technology, maybe, but also by an economy that forces companies to constantly watch profit margins. As we've discussed, fast food companies are a case in point. As much as unions and protesters have tried to improve the situation of workers by insisting on higher wages, those wages are not proving to be much more than a temporary fix. In 2018, for example, McDonald's announced it would roll out self-serve kiosks across the United States (Canadians were already familiar with the machines, as the company had prototyped them north of the border).

Upping the human capital game is easier said than done. It starts, as so many things do, with education, and specifically with getting people to stay enrolled at least through the high school years. In good economic times, the unemployment rate of all groups tends to converge, but during recessions a huge gap opens between the fortunes of those with more education and those with less. During the downturn of 2008–09, for example, the unemployment rate among college-educated workers in the United States never dropped below about 5 percent. For those without a high school diploma, it spiked to over 15 percent.[180] Although we're not necessarily heading into a recession-heavy future, the risk is that the outcomes for less-educated workers will continue to deteriorate, regardless of the economic climate. Of course, as any number of Uber drivers or baristas with advanced degrees will tell you, getting an education is no guarantee that your economic prospects will be everything you've dreamed of. But at the very least, the likelihood of being unemployed decreases as education is acquired.

In large part, preventing people from being involuntary gig workers or getting left on the sidelines by technology involves a broader approach to education. A 2017 report coauthored by Deloitte and Canada's Human Resources Professionals Association urged government and business to work together, suggesting that education reforms are needed to ensure that Canadians enter the workforce with "future-proofed" skills that will allow them to navigate the automated future. One of their recommendations is that schools concentrate more on interdisciplinary work, mental agility, critical thinking, teamwork, relationship management, and the capacity to learn—all "soft" skills similar to those touted by the World Economic Forum and discussed in chapter 5.[181]

Some argue that another way that government can help would-be workers is simply to reduce the cost of third-level education, whether by providing more loans or slashing tuition costs. It is interesting that, in 2018, New York University announced it would be slashing the cost of its medical school from about US$55,000 to zero as a way to make students think less about which specialties would make them enough money to pay back their loans and more about where their skills could be put to good use. In this case, NYU is not a public institution (and the cost of the free tuition is to be borne by donations), but the premise is interesting: If we made education more accessible, would we get better societal outcomes? Perhaps not: perhaps reducing prices would only serve to put more students into areas that interest them, but would not yield skills that are going to be valued by the labor market or truly needed by the economy. It is an interesting premise, though, and one of many possibilities that could occur if we think outside of the box on the way that education should be structured.

Perhaps the most important thing we can do is simply to educate people to the fact that they will constantly have to rethink their jobs and skills over a lifetime, and that the career they entered at age 22 is not the one they should count on having two or three decades later. That may mean full retraining, or it may mean the constant sprucing-up of skills we discussed in chapter 5. To an extent, business has to take a major role in this, but government will also have to play its part. That has always been challenging: governments are rarely credited with doing a great job in taking laid-off factory workers and retraining them for jobs that exist.

To an extent, that is not their fault: often, the laid-off workers do not have the basic skills that would let them be retrained, or they are resistant to the idea. It is, though, a challenge that has to be met if we are going to avoid a future in which people are stuck in long-term unemployment.

Program Reform
Policy reform is also going to need a reset. By and large, the government policies we currently have were meant to go hand in hand with full-time, long-term employment, and the benefits that traditionally came with it. But the times are changing.

As workers make the transition to a more complex economy, governments are naturally going to be under pressure to focus on worker protection. This does not mean moving heaven and earth to make sure that every worker is an old-style employee, which would be akin to trying to cram a square peg into a round hole, but to make sure that workers are not out-and-out exploited (if someone is doing the work of a full-time employee, for example, but has been put on contract simply so that the company can avoid being on the hook for holiday pay or other rights). But what about areas that are a little less black and white, a little more gray? Britain is ahead of the curve on this: in 2018, it implemented a series of laws aimed at providing more rights for workers on online platforms (what they term "vulnerable workers") by making them eligible for holiday and sick pay and granting them the right to request more stable contracts. This followed from a 2016 judgment that reclassified Uber drivers in the U.K. as employees who were entitled to benefits such as sick pay.[182]

There have also been efforts to have online-platform workers in North America classified as employees. In 2018, one high-profile U.S. case involved the food-delivery business Grubhub. A part-time driver (who also worked as an actor) sued the company, claiming that he was basically a part-time employee, and as such had the right to such "perks" as minimum wage, overtime pay, and expenses. The driver lost his case when the judge ruled he was indeed an independent contractor, given that he did not have to go through employee procedures such as wearing a uniform or getting a performance evaluation. However, the judge did acknowledge that many nontraditional workers have attributes of both employees and contractors, and that she was merely ruling on one side rather than the other.[183]

Whether gig workers like the Grubhub driver are employees or not is a debate that will no doubt go on for years. Some decisions may end up going in their favor, and some may go against. The reality, though, is that online platforms represent only a small portion of the gig economy, which means governments will need to tread carefully. Those who work in this space may work in other capacities as well, which makes legislation a challenge. And then there's the fact that many workers *like* being outside of the traditional employment sphere. As we saw in chapter 2, the majority of gig or nontraditional workers either like their work situations or only do gig work in addition to their main jobs. Full-time gig workers (the Reluctants, in the McKinsey parlance) comprise a minority of the total.

No matter how things evolve in terms of protecting workers, we are long past the point—in both the private and public sectors—where being employed means that you never have to think twice about saving for retirement. That's even true for professions like teaching, which in yesteryear provided fairly healthy retirement plans. In fact, the difference between being a teacher in times past and being almost any kind of worker now is stunning.

Take Karen, who became a teacher in the early 1970s (when Richard Nixon was president) and did not retire until a good 30 years later (in the era of George W. Bush). During her career, she worked incredibly, incredibly hard, and gave her all to her students. Finally, though, she was ready to leave the morass that education had become in her state. Paperwork, she explained, took more energy out of her than the kids did, and she found that the stress was getting to her in her 50s in a way it hadn't in her 20s. So it made sense to her to take the offer the state and her union negotiated. She considered her retirement pension fairly modest, and at $75,000 or so a year, perhaps it was. The thing is, if she'd had to generate that kind of income on her own, given the interest rates that prevailed in the early 2000s (and which still prevail), she would have needed to save two to three million dollars on her own. These days, Karen's post-retirement situation is far from guaranteed. There's a real question as to whether school boards will be in a position to continue paying out pensions like the one Karen walked away with. And it's an absolute certainty that those who must provide for themselves will find it increasingly difficult to do so—not impossible, maybe, but certainly a feat that requires a great deal of planning.

What we need now are policies that help workers save for their own retirements, as well for government to educate and encourage them to make sure they do. Programs that let self-employed workers save do exist, but in many cases, their financial situations make it difficult for them to do so. In the United States, for example, just 16 percent of gig workers have a retirement savings plan.[184] That's bad enough, given the number of gig workers we currently have, but it's a disaster in the making if the number of independent workers continues to grow.

Even with the savings vehicles currently available in Canada and the U.S. to help independent workers save for retirement, there is no doubt room for more, and for more creative ways to help them save. In the United States, for example, there are Individual Retirement Accounts (IRAs). One variety allows tax-deductible contributions prior to retirement, and then withdrawals in retirement are taxed; another offers the opposite. In Canada, there are Registered Retirement Savings Plans (RRSPs) and Tax-Free

Savings Accounts (TFSAs). In all cases, there are arguments for raising the contribution limits, and for making it easier for the self-employed or contract workers to use them.

Of course, long before retirement, many future labor-force participants will cope with periods of joblessness, income disruptions (which will affect contract workers at all skill levels), and jobs that pay less than adequate wages, at least for a period of time. Indeed, income volatility, not unemployment, will arguably be the biggest labor issue over the next two decades. A study conducted by Canada's TD Bank in 2017 found that income volatility was indeed a pervasive problem affecting several groups of people, including the self-employed, millennials, and men in their 40s and 50s. Interestingly, the study also found a weak link between education levels and the probability that someone would experience income volatility.[185]

Implementing a basic income could theoretically smooth out income volatility, but it's a very blunt instrument for solving a very specific problem, and probably only a stopgap at that. The real way to deal with income volatility is to encourage people to save for that "rainy day," perhaps by giving them specific incentives to do so, starting very early in their work lives. Maybe this begins by encouraging financial literacy at a young age, but also at more advanced ages as well. And it might include some kind of new "Emergency Savings Fund" that gets a tax break in the short term but also allows for withdrawals long before retirement. An idea like this could be encouraged by both governments and financial institutions.

And what about income support for workers, self-employed or otherwise, not covered by existing government programs? Again, some programs do exist—at least in Canada—but they are not necessarily well used. For example, self-employed Canadians can access maternity benefits if they opt into paying premiums at least a year before they use the benefits. However, those who chose to go this route, and who claim benefits, must continue to pay premiums on their self-employment incomes for the remainder of their careers. It can be worth it for those who plan to follow the Canadian model and take a full year off work, but many who are self-employed don't feel able to do so. As well, none of this really applies to gig workers who may go from one freelance project to another, or to those stringing together a series of part-time and temporary jobs with interruptions in between.

Workers in nontraditional arrangements may never be able to claim unemployment benefits, either, since they do not pay into them the same way as other workers. This is starting to change, slowly. For example, some U.S. states (including Delaware, Maine, Mississippi, New Hampshire, New Jersey, New York, Oregon, Pennsylvania, and Rhode Island) have programs that basically provide unemployment insurance for those working full time to launch their own businesses.[186] An expanded form of this program, to cover other categories of workers beyond business owners, might be one option for offering some worker protections. Governments could also be a player in supporting the idea of "portable" benefits, discussed earlier.

Finally, there is a case to be made that the gig economy itself is acting as a kind of buffer to poverty and an income support to many. It is an idea with merits. If people cannot get a raise in any other way, if they have bills to pay or want to make some money in retirement, then renting out a room or driving an Uber or taking on a few shifts at a restaurant may be a viable option. Clearly, no one is arguing that this type of thing is a substitute for worker protections or proper social programs, but the existence of the gig economy is an asset to many. It may not be ideal, but given the economic turbulence all around us, the existence of this flexible economy may offer some protection to a growing share of the population.

Tough Times for Government Finances

We spend a great deal of time these days talking about what the labor market of the future will do to individuals, but governments should also feel threatened by what is ahead. As well as having to rethink their labor-force strategies in light of automation, demographic shifts, and new working arrangements, they also need to rethink what their revenue streams will look like. The stark reality is that a move to nontraditional work alone would affect government finances; never mind what could happen if a chunk of the population finds itself in a precarious income situation. And the timing could not be worse: those issues will hit government revenues full blast at exactly the same time that an aging population will put a strain on government finances.

It's worth reviewing the challenges that come with an aging population, the same phenomenon that is creating opportunities for some in the labor market. Off the top, as we discussed in chapter 2, the aging population will create slower economic growth. Calculations from the Canadian Department of Finance suggest that, from an average of about 4.8 percent per year before 1990 and about 2.4 percent since, growth in the future could be closer to 1.7 percent. This will logically lead to slower growth in government revenues.[187] As the population ages, fewer people are in the labor force, and therefore are not paying payroll taxes.

There will also be increased pressure on government expenditures: older people simply increase the costs of some government programs. In Canada, the Old Age Security program, which acts as a government pension, is a prime example. According to some estimates, the cost of that program will grow by a whopping 47 percent between 2017 and 2045 as the baby boomers, and in particular the large population cohort born in the mid-1960s, get progressively older. That, of course, is separate from health-care costs, which for Canadians 65 and over in 2014 was 4.5 times higher than it was for those between 15 and 64. Those costs are expected to rise by 57 percent through 2045.[188] Even without the extra burden of labor-market disruptions, those changes alone would create the need for some kind of extra taxation or spending discipline.

On top of all that, consider the potential impact of having more and more people working in some form of nontraditional employment rather than as employees. It's true that if programs are not reformed, there will be some savings to be found: on the payout of employment insurance, for example. But there will also be huge losses in terms of the payroll contributions that typically roll into government coffers. Independent workers are taxed differently than employees, and—without going into a protracted discussion about the tax code in Canada or the United States—by and large at lower rates. Consider also that, in many cases, their earnings are lower than a traditional employee's, and more precarious to boot. Clearly, having a rising share of the population in this category is unlikely to be a positive development for government revenues; nor is raising the tax rates on them likely to be a popular move.

Although there are no good estimates of how much all of this could cost in North America, we can look to Britain to get some sense of it. There, the Trades Union Congress (TUC) estimates that the government is losing £4 billion (about US$5.2 billion) annually as a result of the fact that one in 10 workers is in gig work. Its conclusions are based on the assumption that those employed in the gig economy tend to earn lower incomes than those who are employed at conventional jobs, and so pay less in income tax, and are also more likely to need government benefits such as subsidized housing. Some of this can be addressed by relatively simple policy fixes. For example, in the U.K., self-employed individuals are not subject to the same contributions to national insurance that other employers would be. To be sure, some businesses are constructed specifically to avoid tax. The classic example, as it so often is, is ride-sharing. If it is the driver, a self-employed individual, who is selling the service, the tax treatment is obviously going to be different than if Uber or Lyft is doing the selling and paying wages. This approach is not particularly new—there have always been opportunities to skirt tax rules—but the explosion of the gig economy clearly takes things to a different level. (Britain did make an effort to make up for this in its 2017 budget by increasing national insurance contributions for self-employed workers.)

Indeed, the proliferation of Ubers and the like underline just how far out of date tax policies are in relation to our current industrial structure. In the United States, a study by the Institute on Taxation and Economic Policy has estimated that state and local governments are missing out on $300 million in tax revenues from transportation network companies like Uber as a result of inconsistencies in sales tax policies. A different study, from the Pew Charitable Trusts, found that if Airbnb had to pay the same tax rates as hotels, its tax bill would have been $260 million higher than it was in 2016.[189]

Of course, if governments do go ahead with a universal basic income, the extra costs could be stratospheric. Estimates vary wildly, depending on what assumptions you make, but the net outcome is that any country that goes ahead with a UBI will end up having to finance a big expenditure, one way or another. Bridgewater Associates, the world's largest hedge fund, did some rough calculations of the cost of giving every American $12,000 per year. Their conclusion? Approximately $3.8 trillion annually. To put that into perspective, it's about 21 percent of the U.S. gross domestic product, or 78 percent of all tax revenue.[190]

It's telling that Hillary Clinton, as the candidate for the U.S. Democratic Party in the 2016 presidential campaign, did consider proposing the idea of a basic income as part of her platform. In her campaign memoir, *What Happened,* Clinton says she was inspired by the model used in Alaska, where every state resident gets a check every year, its amount dependent on the state's oil and gas revenues. "I was fascinated by this idea, as was my husband, and we spent weeks working with our policy team to see if it could be viable enough to include in my campaign," she writes. "Unfortunately, we couldn't make the numbers work. To provide a meaningful dividend each year to every citizen, you'd have to raise enormous sums of money, and that would either mean a lot of new taxes or cannibalizing other important programs. We decided it was exciting but not realistic, and left it on the shelf."[191]

All things being equal, we're heading into a future in which the labor market will be continuously evolving. This will be expensive for governments, and will make revenue streams potentially volatile and hard to forecast. The best solution is not likely to come through new taxes, but those may happen anyway. None other than Bill Gates has suggested that we may need a "robot tax" on robot manufacturers that are making machines that displace humans.[192] Whether that ever happens, or whether other taxes are introduced, there is no debate that the challenges ahead will be expensive enough to create a continuous scramble for someone to pay the tab.

TOWARD A BETTER FUTURE

Many books on economic trends end with a chapter on government, with the admonition that government *do* something, and the suggestion that if it spends enough, it can fix the disruptions. There is something to be said for that view: there *are* things that can be done with government help. However, we must also acknowledge that, in this particular phase of labor-force disruption, nothing that government alone can do will be enough. Rather, we are headed for a future in which individuals and business will also have to pitch in. Individuals will need to protect themselves by acquiring education and actively saving and investing against volatility. And business will have to take an active interest in what is happening, both to protect their own short-term interests and to help shape an economy that works over the longer term.

Government should absolutely do something, but it's not going to be effective if it tries to do it alone. A larger partnership, in which everyone buys into the future, will have the best chance of making that future better.

PRECARIOUS WORK OR PORTFOLIO CAREERS?

Let's flash forward to North America in, say, 30 or 40 years, a period of time that will allow those entering college today to be near the end of their careers, or at least contemplating that shift. What kind of work world—or, actually, what kind of world—will they be living in?

Maybe it's one where people pick and choose how they want to work (part-time or full-time; contract, freelance, or permanent), or where they change things up as they see fit, secure in the knowledge that their economic wellbeing is assured. After all, they have the skills and education that allow them to be flexible, and to carve out time with family or for leisure pursuits as they see fit. They are good at managing their finances, and government programs provide a safety net if they need it. Robots are their friends rather than their rivals, and they utilize technology as a tool that helps them and their companies, and allows them to work from various places, rather than just city cores. As a result, the environment is not being destroyed by mass commuting, and real estate prices are not sky-high because everyone wants to live in the same neighborhood. Productivity across the economy is high, so everyone's standard of living is pretty good. Life, actually, is pretty good.

Fairy tale? Sure, but it's a lot more pleasant to imagine a fairy tale than a nightmare. The latter would be a scenario in which unemployment skyrockets because robots are cheap and have learned to do pretty much everyone's job. A working elite does exist, and their lives are pretty sweet. Between the things that robots can do for them (by then, the bots will surely have perfected the art of mixing a sublime martini, whipping up some hors d'oeuvres, and serving it all on a silver tray, with a smile) and their use of cheap and desperate labor, their wish is pretty much everyone's command. For everyone else, things aren't so rosy: grappling for scraps of work, a sliding standard of living, and a government that is hard-pressed to offer an assist.

We've been here before, at an inflection point in terms of how technology, demographics, policy, and attitudes come together to impact the world of work. By and large, the first three industrial revolutions have turned out just fine for workers, and that can be the case this time as well, although maybe not without some speed bumps, and maybe not without an era in which inequality becomes a major issue. But here's the important thing to remember: We are not helpless. We can definitely shape this world and do our best to ensure that it's more fairy tale than nightmare. To do so, though, might necessitate some out-of-the-box thinking, and a realization that clinging to the past is no longer a viable option.

THINKING WAY OUTSIDE OF THE BOX

As a twice-monthly business columnist for the *Globe and Mail*, Canada's national newspaper, I am lucky enough to explore in writing many themes and ideas around labor-force change. The paper allows readers to comment on articles, for good and bad. As anyone who regularly reads such comments knows, they can range from thoughtful and insightful to petty and mean. Sometimes, my articles get a tame reaction, and sometimes they spark a lively debate (such as when I suggested that Prince Harry was "marrying up" because Meghan Markle had an honors university degree while he had skipped out on third-level education). The most dramatic reactions I've ever gotten, though, were for the column about how careers might have to change if we all started living much longer lives.

The piece drew on the work of Dr. Laura Carstensen, director of the Stanford Center on Longevity. Given that people may increasingly live to 80 or 90 or 100, she suggests that we may need to view work more creatively than we've done thus far, and think of it not as something we do intensively for several decades, but as something we dip into and out of over the course of our lives. By stepping in and out of the labor force over a long period of time, people would grow accustomed to the idea of working into their senior years; in turn, this approach might also allow them to spend more time in non-work-related pursuits when they are young—traveling, volunteering, spending time with children, et cetera. Dr. Carstensen has even mulled over a radical concept, one I shared with *Globe and Mail* readers: maybe for some people, full-time work should start at the age of 40.[193] Granted, this might not be a realistic path for many people, but it was an interesting idea, and I wanted to put it out there. The reaction was also interesting, to say the least.

Predictably, many people called me crazy and suggested that I was not fit to write a column; one said he had seen a similar plot on *Star Trek*. A few people hurled the worst insult they could think of, which was to call me either a "crazy left-winger" or a "crazy right-winger." (I'm still trying to figure out how I could possibly be both!) More practically, many readers pointed out that if you have a family, you have to support it, so there really were few options besides working flat out through your 20s and 30s.

One of the most thoughtful comments came from an older woman who took the time to really ponder the prospect. She said that she sometimes thinks it might have made sense to have been home with her kids when she was in her 30s, and then to have gone full blast in her career when she was a little older. And, of course, that is what many, although certainly not all, women have chosen to do. With young women and young men now more likely to be earning similar salaries, maybe it is an option—just an option—for men as well. Or maybe not. The point is simply this: there are many, many work and life paths available to people, and perhaps it makes sense to think about them (even if it does mean thinking "like a girl" on occasion). After all, technology and science, including the science that is allowing us to live longer lives, is already way out of the box. Maybe it's time we followed.

ALL HANDS ON DECK

So, here we are, looking at that messy, promising future. To navigate it, we need government and business to be partners. Perhaps more importantly, we need individuals to be active participants, too, and active in more ways than just going to work. It would be naive to think that all the trends are working in everyone's favor: they are not. As we've seen, the big paybacks will be to those with flexibility, the ability to pivot, and the mix of hard and soft skills that will be valued by the future labor market. For sure, it is a future that could be all about divergences: between incomes and prospects and working conditions and lives. And yet, it need not be.

The very worst way to approach that future is to be the individual looking for a better payback on the lower-income jobs that now exist. Forget being a taxi driver, or even a driver for Uber or Lyft; by the time we get to our imagined future, driverless cars will be the norm. Working in a factory or even in an Amazon fulfillment center may not be a viable option either. If those jobs, or jobs like them, do still exist, they're likely becoming more precarious and poorly paid by the day (which is why it makes no sense for government to put efforts into trying to hold on to those specific job functions; their time and money could be much better spent).

The good news is that if we do shift to that higher-productivity economy, the one where technology is used in the right way, the jobs that exist will pay better and offer better options in terms of when and where they are done. We see glimpses of that future already, in the portfolio careers that some are embracing, or in the vacation policies that let people alternate working flat out on a project with hanging with the giant tortoises in the Galapagos Islands, or maybe just hanging with their kids on a more flexible schedule.

If that scenario sounds like a *Star Trek* fantasy, let's remind ourselves that the technology we have now in many ways outpaces anything that the television producers of the 1960s could have imagined. We have created a world in which it seems like everyone in North America has a smartphone that lets them take pictures and post them on the internet, and play Pokémon Quest on demand. Why, then, is it so radical to think that we can harness technology in a way that gives us things we can really use, like a better quality of life and an end to poverty?

We have been here before and we have come out better. Having a job may not mean the same thing in 40 years that it does now, or that it did 40 years ago, but that can be all to the good. As a society, we can line up training to make ourselves winners in the world that is emerging. We can craft policies that will ensure a safety net if and when one is needed. And we can rethink our lives to function around a world of work rather than a world of jobs. So, let's go ahead and really imagine our lives and our organizations and the post-jobs economy. Let's imagine an amazing future, one in which people are engaged and working and satisfied and well compensated. And then, let's go out and create it.

ACKNOWLEDGMENTS

This book is the result of years of not just researching and observing the labor market, but of interacting with people across a wide range of industries, occupations, and locations. As a keynote speaker, I am so fortunate to be able to share my insights, and to frequently have my audiences share theirs with me as well. So, off the top, a huge thank you to everyone who has ever done that, or who has sent an email or a tweet or left a comment sharing their work experiences, whether in a traditional or nontraditional workplace. Please keep the comments coming: you can visit me at www.relentlesseconomics.com and send me a note any time.

Thank you, too, to all the companies and organizations that have invited me to share my thoughts with their audiences. There are too many to mention individually, but a special shout-out goes to the Conference Board of Canada, to whom I gave the first "Work Is Not a Place" presentation while still in the early stages of writing.

Many people shared their experiences with me expressly for this book, and they have my gratitude for being so generous with their time and thoughts on both the work world and on economic transformation in general. In particular, I thank Marci Alboher, Amy Laski, Tracey Malcolm, Mark Matulis, Shashank Nigam, Jason Peetsma, Andrew Stoakley, and Wendy Waters.

A very special thank you goes to David Foot, who not only helped me get my first job in economics (so many years ago), but who also inspired me and so many others to believe that demographics explains two-thirds of everything. He was generous enough to read some of this book and offer comments (including healthy disagreements with some things), but he is in no way responsible for any deficiencies in its content.

Many of the topics covered here were also covered in my bimonthly column in Canada's *Globe and Mail*. Accordingly, my thanks go to the paper (and particularly to my editor, Aron Yeomanson) for giving me the chance to explore so many fascinating topics related to the work world. I also have benefited from my association with the Macdonald-Laurier Institute, and wish to particularly thank Brian Lee Crowley for inviting me to be a senior fellow at this much-respected think tank.

This is my second foray into "artisanal publishing," and I am so grateful to once again have had the chance to work with editor Linda Pruessen, who guided this work from the beginning. Lloyd Davis also offered able editorial assistance later on; Jana Rade of impact studios provided a terrific cover; and Tracy Lamourie of Lamourie PR continues to bring her energy to the project.

Finally, to Lou and Maddie: you guys are awesome, and I thank you for just being you.

ENDNOTES

Introduction

[1] Jim Harter, "Dismal Employee Engagement Is a Sign of Global Mismanagement," Gallup, http://www.gallup.com/workplace/231668/dismal-employee-engagement-sign-global-mismanagement.aspx.

[2] "Why Loneliness Can Be as Unhealthy as Smoking 15 Cigarettes a Day," CBC News, August 16, 2017, http://www.cbc.ca/news/health/loneliness-public-health-psychologist-1.4249637.

Chapter 1

"Cottage Industry and the Industrial Revolution," *Mazzmanali* (blog), https://mazzmanali.wordpress.com/2013/04/12/cottage-industry-and-the-industrial-revolution/.

[4] "Cottage Industry and the Industrial Revolution," *Mazzmanali* (blog), https://mazzmanali.wordpress.com/2013/04/12/cottage-industry-and-the-industrial-revolution/.

[5] C.W., "Did Living Standards Improve During the Industrial Revolution?" *The Economist*, September 13, 2013, https://www.economist.com/blogs/freeexchange/2013/09/economic-history-0.

[6] "The History of Benefits," WorkPlace Consultants, http://workplaceconsultants.net/commentary/retirementtsunami/the-history-of-benefits/.

[7] Kate Taylor, "Ikea Has Acquired TaskRabbit—and It Could Fix the Most Annoying Thing about the Furniture Giant," *Business Insider*, September 28, 2017, http://www.businessinsider.com/report-ikea-acquires-taskrabbit-2017-9.

[8] "Ford Crisis of 1920–1921," Strategos, http://www.strategosinc.com/ford_crises.htm.

[9] Ian Bickis, "Leaner Oilpatch Emerges from Recession as New Technology Replaces Jobs," CBC News, March 1, 2017, http://www.cbc.ca/news/canada/calgary/oilpatch-downturn-technology-advances-replace-jobs-automation-1.4004855.

10 Giorgio Biscardini, Reid Morrison, David Branson, and Adrian del Maestro, "2017 Oil and Gas Trends," *Strategy&*, https://www.strategyand.pwc.com/trend/2017-oil-and-gas-trends.

11 "Median Age," *World Factbook* (Washington, DC: Central Intelligence Agency), https://www.cia.gov/library/publications/the-world-factbook/fields/2177.html.

12 "The 10 Most Popular Ice Cream Brands in India," *Trending Top Most*, http://www.trendingtopmost.com/worlds-popular-list-top-10/2017-2018-2019-2020-2021/foods/most-popular-ice-cream-brands-india-best-selling/.

13 Staff, "The Retreat of the Global Economy," *The Economist*, January 28, 2017, https://www.economist.com/news/briefing/21715653-biggest-business-idea-past-three-decades-deep-trouble-retreat-global.

14 Gerald Davis, "Post-Corporate: The Disappearing Corporation in the New Economy," *Third Way*, February 1, 2017, http://www.thirdway.org/report/post-corporate-the-disappearing-corporation-in-the-new-economy.

15 Chris Isidore, "Jeff Bezos Is the Richest Person in History," CNN, January 9, 2018, http://money.cnn.com/2018/01/09/technology/jeff-bezos-richest/index.html.

16 Alexandra Scaggs, "On Juggernaut Companies and Wage Growth," *Financial Times*, February 9, 2018, https://ftalphaville.ft.com/2018/02/08/1518119813000/On-juggernaut-companies-and-wage-growth/.

17 Guy Burtless, "Unemployment and the 'Skills Mismatch' Story: Overblown and Unpersuasive," Brookings, July 29, 2014, https://www.brookings.edu/opinions/unemployment-and-the-skills-mismatch-story-overblown-and-unpersuasive/.

18 Cade Metz, "Tech Giants Are Paying Huge Salaries for Scarce A.I. Talent," *New York Times*, October 22, 2017, https://www.nytimes.com/2017/10/22/technology/artificial-intelligence-experts-salaries.html.

Chapter 2

19 Forster, Tim, "Quebec Fast Food Chains Face Staff Shortage", *Eater Montreal*, September 19, 2017, https://montreal.eater.com/2017/9/19/16334470/quebec-fast-food-restaurants-labour-shortage-unemployment.

20 There are several reasons for the baby boom, including the fact that the those who had put off marriage during the Depression and World War II started having children in the years following the war—at the same time that a younger cohort were doing so.

[21] Crystal Schwanke, "Baby Boomer Statistics," *Love to Know*, https://seniors.lovetoknow.com/Baby_Boomer_Statistics.

[22] Statistics Canada, "Generations in Canada," *The Canadian Population in 2011: Age and Sex* (98-311-X-2011003), http://www12.statcan.gc.ca/census-recensement/2011/as-sa/98-311-x/98-311-x2011003_2-eng.cfm.

[23] Statistics Canada, "Generations in Canada," *The Canadian Population in 2011: Age and Sex* (98-311-X-2011003), http://www12.statcan.gc.ca/census-recensement/2011/as-sa/98-311-x/98-311-x2011003_2-eng.cfm.

[24] Statistics Canada, "Fertility: Fewer Children, Older Moms," *The Daily*, May 17, 2018, https://www.statcan.gc.ca/pub/11-630-x/11-630-x2014002-eng.htm.

[25] Statistics Canada puts the Baby Bust years as happening between 1966 and 1971 ("Generations in Canada," *The Canadian Population in 2011: Age and Sex* [98-311-X-2011003], http://www12.statcan.gc.ca/census-recensement/2011/as-sa/98-311-x/98-311-x2011003_2-eng.cfm.

[26] Statistics Canada, "Population Estimates on July 1st, by Age and Sex," Table 17-10-0005-01 (formerly CANSIM 051-0001), https://www150.statcan.gc.ca/t1/tbl1/en/tv.action?pid=1710000501.

[27] "Median Age," *World Factbook* (Washington, DC: Central Intelligence Agency), https://www.cia.gov/library/publications/the-world-factbook/fields/2177.html.

[28] "Working in the 21st Century," U.S. Bureau of Labor Statistics, https://www.bls.gov/opub/working/page1b.htm.

[29] Statistics Canada, "Labour Force Characteristics by Sex and Detailed Age Group (Annual)," Table 14-10-0018-01 (formerly CANSIM 282-0002), https://www150.statcan.gc.ca/t1/tbl1/en/tv.action?pid=1410001801; author calculations also used.

[30] Samanthan Raphelson, "Trucking Industry Struggles with Growing Driver Shortage," NPR, January 9, 2018, https://www.npr.org/2018/01/09/576752327/trucking-industry-struggles-with-growing-driver-shortage.

[31] Employment and Social Development Canada, "Canadian Occupation Projection System (COPS)," Government of Canada, October 3, 2017, http://occupations.esdc.gc.ca/sppc-cops/w.2lc.4m.2@-eng.jsp.

[32] Rebecca Grant, "The U.S. Is Running Out of Nurses," *The Atlantic*, February 3, 2016, https://www.theatlantic.com/health/archive/2016/02/nursing-shortage/459741/.

[33] Clive Crook, "Full Employment," Bloomberg, July 6, 2018, https://www.bloomberg.com/quicktake/full-employment

34 Robert Solow, "We'd Better Watch Out," *New York Times Book Review*, July 12, 1987, page 36.

35 Alex Verkhiver, "Why the AI Boom Isn't Boosting Productivity," *Chicago Booth Review*, March 5, 2018, http://review.chicagobooth.edu/economics/2018/article/why-ai-boom-isn-t-boosting-productivity.

36 Jen St. Denis, "Productivity Growth Continues to Slow in Canada: OECD," *BIV*, May 26, 2016, https://biv.com/article/2016/05/productivity-growth-slows-canada.

37 Department of Finance, "Update of Long-Term Economic and Fiscal Projections 2017," Government of Canada, https://www.fin.gc.ca/pub/ltefp-peblt/2017/report-rapport-eng.asp.

38 "Labor Force Projections to 2024: The Labor Force is Growing, But Slowly," U.S. Bureau of Labor Statistics, December 2015, https://www.bls.gov/opub/mlr/2015/article/labor-force-projections-to-2024.htm.

39 Gordon Hanson, Chen Liu, Craig McIntosh, "Along the Watchtower: The Rise and Fall of U.S. Low-Skilled Immigration," *Brookings Papers on Economic Activity, BPEA Conference Drafts*, March 23–24, 2017, https://www.brookings.edu/wp-content/uploads/2017/03/2_hansonetal.pdf.

40 "Countries by Median Age 2018," World Population Review, http://worldpopulationreview.com/countries/median-age/.

41 Danielle Demetriou, "Japanese Couple Apologise for Ignoring Work Pregnancy Timetable by Conceiving 'Before Their Turn,'" *The Telegraph*, April 2, 2018, https://www.telegraph.co.uk/news/2018/04/03/japanese-couple-apologise-ignoring-work-pregnancy-timetable/.

42 Dan Kopf, "Older Women Are Saving Japan's Economy," *Quartz*, July 24, 2017, https://qz.com/1036377/the-dramatic-rise-in-older-women-working-in-japan/.

43 Bruce Shutan, "Rhino Foods Serves Up Creative Benefits for Workers," *Employee Benefit News*, February 15, 2018, https://www.benefitnews.com/news/vt-broker-serves-creative-benefits-for-rhino-foods.

44 Bruce Shutan, "Rhino Foods Serves Up Creative Benefits for Workers," *Employee Benefit News*, February 15, 2018, https://www.benefitnews.com/news/vt-broker-serves-creative-benefits-for-rhino-foods.

45 Jim Mendoza, "Big Island Coffee Farms Face a New Threat: A Labor Shortage," *Hawaii News Now*, February 17, 2018, http://www.hawaiinewsnow.com/story/37527628/big-island-coffee-farms-face-a-new-threat-a-labor-shortage.

46 Jacob Serebrin, "Too Few Cooks: Quebec Restaurants Facing a Labour Shortage," *Montreal Gazette*, January 29, 2018, http://montrealgazette.com/business/local-business/too-few-cooks-quebec-restaurants-facing-a-labour-shortage.

[47] Mai Chi Dao, Mitali Das, Zsoka Koczan, and Weichang Lian, "Drivers of Declining Labor Share of Income," *IMFBlog*, April 12, 2017, https://blogs.imf.org/2017/04/12/drivers-of-declining-labor-share-of-income/.

[48] Deirdre Wang Morris, "China's Aging Population Threatens Its Manufacturing Might," CNBC, October 24, 2012, https://www.cnbc.com/id/49498720.

[49] Charles Goodhart and Manoj Pradhan, "Demographics Will Reverse Three Multi-Decade Global Trends," Bank for International Settlements, *BIS Working Papers No. 656* (August 2017), https://www.bis.org/publ/work656.pdf.

Chapter 3

[50] John G. Messerly, "Aristotle, Robot Slaves and a New Economic System," Institute for Ethics and Emerging Technologies, May 27, 2015, https://ieet.org/index.php/IEET2/more/messerly20150527.

[51] Peter F. Drucker, "The Age of Social Transformation," *Atlantic Monthly*, December 1995, http://www.theatlantic.com/past/docs/issues/95dec/chilearn/drucker.htm.

[52] The definition of the industrial revolutions comes from the World Economic Forum. Others use slightly different definitions and years.

[53] Michael J. Coren, "Luddites Have Been Getting a Bad Rap for 200 Years. But, Turns Out, They Were Right," *Quartz*, April 30, 2017, https://qz.com/968692/luddites-have-been-getting-a-bad-rap-for-200-years-but-turns-out-they-were-right/.

[54] John Maynard Keynes, "Economic Possibilities for Our Grandchildren," http://www.econ.yale.edu/smith/econ116a/keynes1.pdf.

[55] James Bessen, "How Technology Has Affected Wages for the Last 200 Years," *Harvard Business Review*, April 29, 2015, https://hbr.org/2015/04/how-technology-has-affected-wages-for-the-last-200-years.

[56] "Living and Working Conditions, 1815–1851," BBC, https://www.bbc.com/bitesize/guides/zwdqk7h/revision/4.

[57] Klaus Schwab, "The Fourth Industrial Revolution: What It Means, How to Respond," World Economic Forum, January 14, 2016, https://www.weforum.org/agenda/2016/01/the-fourth-industrial-revolution-what-it-means-and-how-to-respond/.

[58] Matt Grasser, "The Fourth Industrial Revolution," *Next Billion*, January 30, 2017, https://nextbillion.net/the-fourth-industrial-revolution-how-big-data-and-machine-learning-can-boost-inclusive-fintech/.

59   Tina Hesman Saey, "New Genetic Sleuthing Tools Helped Track Down the Golden State Killer Suspect," *ScienceNews*, April 29, 2018, https://www.sciencenews.org/article/golden-state-killer-suspect-dna-genetics-genealogy.

60   Data are from the Current Population Survey from the U.S. Census Bureau, and were provided by special request of the author.

61   U.S. Bureau of Labor Statistics, "Employment by Major Industry Sector," October 24, 2017, https://www.bls.gov/emp/tables/employment-by-major-industry-sector.htm, and U.S. Bureau of Labor Statistics data retrieved from Federal Reserve of St. Louis Database (FRED).

62   Charles Kenny, "Why Factory Jobs are Shrinking Everywhere," Bloomberg, April 28, 2014, http://www.bloomberg.com/news/articles/2014-04-28/why-factory-jobs-are-shrinking-everywhere.

63   Eric Brynjolffson, and Andrew McAfee, *Race Against the Machine: How the Digital Revolution Is Accelerating Innovation, Driving Productivity, and Irreversibly Transforming Employment and the Economy* (Lexington, MA: Digital Frontier Press, 2011).

64   Amy Bernstein and Anand Raman, "The Great Decoupling: An Interview With Eric Brynjolfsson and Andrew McAfee," *Harvard Business Review*, June 2015.

65   Connor Forrest, "Chinese Factory Replaces 90% of Humans with Robots, Production Soars," *TechRepublic*, July 30, 2015, https://www.techrepublic.com/article/chinese-factory-replaces-90-of-humans-with-robots-production-soars/.

66   Australia, Brazil, China, France, Germany, India, Italy, Japan, Mexico, South Africa, Turkey, the United Kingdom, and the United States, plus the ASEAN (Association of Southeast Asian Countries) and GCC (Gulf Cooperation Council) groups.

67   World Economic Forum, "The Future of Jobs: Employment, Skills and Workforce Strategy for the Fourth Industrial Revolution," *Global Challenge Insight Report*, January 2016, http://www3.weforum.org/docs/WEF_Future_of_Jobs.pdf.

68   Andy Haldane, "Labour's Share," speech by the chief economist of the Bank of England, at the British Trades Union Congress, November 12, 2015.

69   Daron Acemoglu and Pascual Restrepo, "Robots and Jobs: Evidence from US Labor Markets," *NBER Working Paper No 23285*, National Bureau of Economic Research, March 2017, http://www.nber.org/papers/w23285.

70 "Consumer Spending Prospects and the Impact of Automation on Jobs," PwC, UK Economic Outlook, March 2017, http://www.pwc.co.uk/services/economics-policy/insights/uk-economic-outlook.html.

71 James Manyika, Michael Chui, Mehdi Miremade, Jacques Bughin, et al., "A Future That Works: Automation, Employment and Productivity," McKinsey Global Institute, January 2017, https://www.mckinsey.com/mgi/overview/2017-in-review/automation-and-the-future-of-work/a-future-that-works-automation-employment-and-productivity.

72 Fred Wang, "Racing Towards the Precipice," Brookings, June 1, 2012, https://www.brookings.edu/articles/racing-towards-the-precipice/.

73 As quoted in Julia Limitone, "Frm. McDonald's USA CEO: $35K Robot Cheaper Than Hiring at $15 Per Hour," FoxBusiness, May 24, 2016, http://www.foxbusiness.com/features/2016/05/24/fmr-mcdonalds-usa-ceo-35k-robots-cheaper-than-hiring-at-15-per-hour.html.

74 As quoted in Tim Worstall, "Wendy's Explains What Really Happens with a Minimum Raise Rise: Job Losses," *Forbes*, August 11, 2015, http://www.forbes.com/sites/timworstall/2015/08/11/wendys-explains-what-really-happens-with-a-minimum-wage-rise-job-losses/#4b59baad8dc3.

75 "Automation, Jobs, and the Future of Work," McKinsey Global Institute, December 2014, http://www.mckinsey.com/global-themes/employment-and-growth/automation-jobs-and-the-future-of-work.

76 John Lieber and Lucas Puente, "Beyond the Gig Economy: How New Technologies are Shaping the Future of Work," *Thumbtack Journal*, March 9, 2016, https://www.thumbtack.com/blog/beyond-the-gig-economy/.

77 Carl Benedikt Frey and Michael Osborne, "The Future of Employment: How Susceptible Are Jobs to Computerisation?" working paper, Oxford Martin School, University of Oxford, London, UK, September 17, 2013.

78 Council of Economic Advisers, "Economic Report of the President," February 2016, https://www.whitehouse.gov/sites/default/files/docs/ERP_2016_Book_Complete%20JA.pdf.

79 Ljubica Nedelkoska and Glenda Quintini, "Automation, Skills Use and Training," *OECD Social, Employment and Migration Working Papers, No. 202* (Paris: OECD Publishing, 2018), http://dx.doi.org/10.1787/2e2f4eea-en.

80 David H. Autor, "Polanyi's Paradox and the Shape of Employment Growth," Massachusetts Institute of Technology, September 2014, http://economics.mit.edu/files/9835.

81 Greg Toppo, "Why You Might Want to Think Twice About Going to Law School," *USA Today*, June 28, 2017, https://www.usatoday.com/story/news/2017/06/28/law-schools-hunkering-down-enrollment-slips/430213001/.

82 Thomas S. Clay and Eric A. Seeger, *Law Firms in Transition* (Newtown Square, PA: Atman Weil, 2015), http://www.altmanweil.com/dir_docs/resource/1c789ef2-5cff-463a-863a-2248d23882a7_document.pdf.

83 Jill Treanor, "Banking Is Facing Its 'Uber Moment' Says Former Barclays Boss," *The Guardian*, November 25, 2015, https://www.theguardian.com/business/2015/nov/25/banking-facing-uber-moment-says-former-barclays-boss.

84 Telis Demos, "Citi: Technology Could Cost 2 Million Bank Employees Their Jobs," *Wall Street Journal*, March 30, 2016, http://blogs.wsj.com/moneybeat/2016/03/30/citi-technology-could-cost-two-million-bank-employees-their-jobs/.

85 Georg Graetz and Guy Michaels, "Robots at Work," *CEP Discussion Paper No. 1335*, March 2015, http://cep.lse.ac.uk/pubs/download/dp1335.pdf.

Chapter 4

86 Belinda Luscombe, "There Is No Longer any Such Thing as a Typical Family," *Time*, September 4, 2014, http://time.com/3265733/nuclear-family-typical-society-parents-children-households-philip-cohen/.

87 "Gig Economy," Investopedia, https://www.investopedia.com/terms/g/gig-economy.asp.

88 Patrick Gillespie, "Intuit: Gig Economy is 24% of US Workforce," CNN Money, May 24, 2017, http://money.cnn.com/2017/05/24/news/economy/gig-economy-intuit/index.html.

89 Robert McGuire, "Ultimate Guide to Gig Economy Data: A Summary of Every Freelance Survey We Can Find," *Nation 1099*, July 16, 2018, http://nation1099.com/gig-economy-data-freelancer-study/.

90 "Workforce 2025," Randstad, http://content.randstad.ca/hubfs/workforce2025/Workforce-2025-Randstad-Part1.pdf.

91 James Manyika, Susan Lund, Jacques Bughin, Kelsey Robinson, Jan Mischke, and Deepa Mahajan, "Independent Work: Choice, Necessity, and the Gig Economy," McKinsey Global Institute, October 2016, https://www.mckinsey.com/global-themes/employment-and-growth/independent-work-choice-necessity-and-the-gig-economy.

92 Tim Talley, Melissa Daniels, Michael Melia, and John Raby, "'I Just Have to Do It.' Teachers Struggle with Second Jobs," Associated Press, April 15, 2018, http://www.660news.com/2018/04/15/i-just-have-to-do-it-teachers-struggle-with-second-jobs/.

93 "Rural Teachers Working Second Jobs, Struggling to Make Ends Meet," CBSDenver, April 26, 2018, http://denver.cbslocal.com/2018/04/26/rural-teachers-struggling-school-funding/.

94 Izzy Best, "Etsy for Teachers? TpT Becomes Hub for Education Materials," CNBC, October 22, 2015, https://www.cnbc.com/2015/10/09/teacherspayteachers-a-hub-for-education-materials.html.

95 Maria Puente, "Queen Elizabeth II Rakes in Whopping $9M Racing Her Beloved Horses," *USA Today*, March 7, 2018, https://www.usatoday.com/story/life/2018/03/07/queen-elizabeth-ii-rakes-whopping-9-m-racing-her-beloved-horses/400888002/.

96 Some names have been changed.

97 John Rampton, "Are Freelancers Happier than Traditional Workers?" *Inc.*, July 30, 2017, https://www.inc.com/john-rampton/are-freelancers-happier-than-traditional-workers.html.

98 Rick Wartzman, "Working in the Gig Economy Is Both Desirable and Detestable," *Fortune*, April 27, 2016, http://fortune.com/2016/04/27/uber-gig-economy/.

99 Jody Greenstone Miller and Matt Miller, "The Rise of the Supertemp," *Harvard Business Review*, May 2012, https://hbr.org/2012/05/the-rise-of-the-supertemp.

100 Lucy Bielby, "How Can an Interim Add Value to Your Business?" *Executives Online*, January 8, 2018, http://blog.executivesonline.co.uk/blog/how-can-an-interim-add-value.

101 Tam Harbert, "Tech Pros Make the Most of the 'Gig Economy,'" *Computerworld*, September 8, 2015, https://www.computerworld.com/article/2979718/it-careers/tech-pros-make-the-most-of-the-gig-economy.html.

102 Alison DeNisco Rayome, "The 10 Highest-Paying Gig Economy Jobs Are All in Tech," *TechRepublic*, March 13, 2018, https://www.techrepublic.com/article/the-10-highest-paying-gig-economy-jobs-are-all-in-tech/.

103 *The 2016 Field Nation Freelancer Study: The Changing Face of the New Blended Workforce*, Field Nation, https://fieldnation.com/wp-content/uploads/2017/03/The_2016_Field_Nation_Freelancer_Study_R1V1__1_-2.pdf.

104 Alana Semuels, "This Is What Life Without Retirement Savings Looks Like," *The Atlantic*, February 22, 2018, https://www.theatlantic.com/business/archive/2018/02/pensions-safety-net-california/553970/.

105 Helen Holmes, "Folding Underwear, Walking Dogs, and Building Furniture: My Journey into the Gig Economy," *Glamour*, May 8, 2018, https://www.glamour.com/story/gig-economy.

106 Fionn Rogan, "Gig Economy Is the Mass Exploitation of Millennials," *Irish Times*, Febuary 5, 2018, https://www.irishtimes.com/opinion/gig-economy-is-the-mass-exploitation-of-millennials-1.3379569.

107   Hannah Jane Parkinson, "'Sometimes You Don't Feel Human'—How the Gig Economy Chews Up and Spits Out Millennials," *The Guardian*, October 17, 2017, https://www.theguardian.com/business/2017/oct/17/sometimes-you-dont-feel-human-how-the-gig-economy-chews-up-and-spits-out-millennials.

108   Valerie Calderon, "US Students' Entrepreneurial Energy Waiting to Be Tapped," Gallup, October 13, 2011, http://news.gallup.com/poll/150077/Students-Entrepreneurial-Energy-Waiting-Tapped.aspx.

Chapter 5

109   Brian Bell, "New Study Finds Trump Voters Motivated by Fear of Losing Status, Rather Than Economic Anxiety," *Paste*, April 24, 2018, https://www.pastemagazine.com/articles/2018/04/new-study-finds-trump-voters-motivated-by-fear-of.html.

110   Chad Brooks, "Robots and Changing Job Skills Are Stressing Your Employees Out," *Business News Daily*, June 6, 2017, https://www.business-newsdaily.com/9986-employee-stress-factors.html.

111   Susanna Loeb, "The Financial Stress of Teaching in Regions of Fast Economic Growth," Brookings, May 10, 2018, https://www.brookings.edu/research/the-financial-stress-of-teaching-in-regions-of-fast-economic-growth/.

112   Lisa Pickoff-White and Ryan Levi, "Are There Really More Dogs Than Children in S.F.?" KQED News, May 24, 2018, https://www.kqed.org/news/11669269/are-there-really-more-dogs-than-children-in-s-f.

113   P.C. Patel, S. Devarag, Michael Hicks, Emily Wornell, "County-Level Job Automation Risk and Health: Evidence from the United States," *Social Science & Medicine* 202 (April 2018): 54–60, https://www.sciencedirect.com/science/article/pii/S0277953618300819?via%253dihub.

114   Mitchell Hartman, "What Makes Gig Economy Workers Anxious," *Marketplace*, March 8, 2018, https://www.marketplace.org/2018/03/08/economy/anxiety-index/gig-workers-and-economically-anxious-lifestyle.

115   Julia Sklar, "Robots Lay Three Times as Many Bricks as Construction Workers," *MIT Technology Review*, September 2, 2015, https://www.technologyreview.com/s/540916/robots-lay-three-times-as-many-bricks-as-construction-workers/.

116   Kendall Jones, "Will Robots & Automation Replace Construction Workers," *ConstructConnect*, February 2, 2018, https://www.constructconnect.com/blog/construction-technology/will-robots-automation-replace-construction-workers/.

117 Jacques Bughin, Eric Hazan, Susan Lund, Peter Dahlström, Anna Wiesinger, Amrash Subramaniam, "Skill Shift: Automation and the Future of the Workforce," McKinsey Global Institute (discussion paper), May 2018, "https://www.mckinsey.com/~/media/mckinsey/global%20 themes/future%20of%20organizations/skill%20shift%20automation%20and%20the%20future%20of%20the%20workforce/mgi-skill-shift-automation-and-future-of-the-workforce-may-2018.ashx.

118 Steve LeVine, "Forget About Broad-Based Pay Hikes, Executives Say," Axios, May 27, 2018, https://www.axios.com/broad-based-pay-rises-retraining-automation-executives-3e68d31c-51bc-4bde-a362-7ce12b039e7c.html.

119 Robert Booth, "700,000 Gig Workers Paid Below National Minimum Wage," *The Guardian*, February 7, 2018, https://www.theguardian.com/ business/2018/feb/07/death-dpd-courier-don-lane-tragedy-business-secretary.

120 "Gig Workers in America," Prudential Insurance Company of America, 2017, http://research.prudential.com/documents/rp/Gig_Economy_ Whitepaper.pdf.

121 "MBO Partners State of Independence in America 2018," MBO Partners, 2018, https://www.mbopartners.com/state-of-independence.

122 "Millions of Canadians Impacted by Income Volatility: TD," Ipsos, May 18, 2017, https://www.ipsos.com/en-ca/news-polls/millions-canadians-impacted-income-volatility-td.

123 Elizabeth Mulholland, "We Need to Act on Income Volatility Now," HuffPost, May 24, 2017, https://www.huffingtonpost.ca/elizabeth-mulholland/income-volatility-canada_b_16785476.html.

124 "OECD PISA Financial Literacy Assessment of Students," OECD, 2018, http://www.oecd.org/finance/financial-education/oecdpisafinancialliteracyassessment.htm.

125 Peter Balonon-Rosen and Kimberley Adams, "Women and the Gig Economy: 'Every Job You Have Is Essentially the Last One,'" *Marketplace*, March 23, 2018, https://www.marketplace.org/2018/03/23/economy/ anxiety-index/every-job-you-have-essentially-last-one-women-and-gig-economy.

126 John Swanciger, "Going Solo in the Gig Economy? How to Work Alone without Feeling Lonely," *Inc.*, September 29, 2017, https://www.inc.com/ john-swanciger/going-solo-in-gig-economy-how-to-work-alone-without-feeling-lonely.html.

127 Okanagan Colab, "Kelowna's Largest Coworking Space Soubles Capacity," coLab, March 3, 2017, http://okcolab.com/kelownas-largest-coworking-space-doubles-capacity/.

Chapter 6

128 "Strategic planning," BusinessDictionary, http://www.businessdictionary.com/definition/strategic-planning.html.

129 Scott Keller and Mary Meaney, "Attracting and Retaining the Right Talent," McKinsey & Company, November 2017, https://www.mckinsey.com/business-functions/organization/our-insights/attracting-and-retaining-the-right-talent.

130 David Cyranoski, "China Enters the Battle for AI Talent" *Nature*, January 15, 2018, https://www.nature.com/articles/d41586-018-00604-6.

131 Douglas Quan, "As Vancouver Tried to Woo Amazon, Staff Fretted over Housing Data That Could Make City 'Look Bad,'" *National Post*, June 17, 2018, http://nationalpost.com/news/canada/as-vancouver-tried-to-woo-amazon-staff-fretted-over-housing-data-that-could-make-city-look-bad.

132 "Korn Ferry Study Reveals Company Payrolls Could Soar Long-Term Due to Global Skilled Talent Shortages," Korn Ferry, June 20, 2018, https://www.kornferry.com/press/company-payrolls-could-soar-long-term-due-to-global-skilled-talent-shortages/.

133 Don Rheem, "ForbesBook AuthorVoice: This One Thing Can Immediately Improve Productivity and Trust in the Workplace," *Forbes*, June 1, 2018,

https://www.forbes.com/sites/forbesbooksauthors/2018/06/01/this-one-thing-can-immediately-improve-productivity-and-trust-in-the-workplace/#2dcb98324d5c.

134 "Work-Life Imbalance: Expedia's 2016 Vacation Deprivation Study Shows Americans Leave Hundreds of Millions of Paid Vacation Days Unused," *Expedia Viewfinder*, November 15, 2016, viewfinder.expedia.com/news/work-life-imbalance-expedias-2016-vacation-deprivation-study-shows-americans-leave-hundreds-millions-paid-vacation-days-unused.

135 "Does the Open Plan Office Work?" Sage, https://www.sage.com/za/business-resources/essential-reading/does-the-open-plan-office-work-infographic.

136 "Does the Open Plan Office Work?" Sage, https://www.sage.com/za/business-resources/essential-reading/does-the-open-plan-office-work-infographic.

137 Melia Robinson, "LinkedIn Took Over a 26-Story San Francisco Skyscraper, and It's Unlike Anything Else We've Seen," *Business Insider*, May 2, 2017, http://www.businessinsider.com/linkedin-office-tour-san-francisco-2017-4.

138 Pamela DeLoatch, "For Real Engagement, Show Employees Where They Fit In," *HRDive*, June 11, 2018, https://www.hrdive.com/news/for-real-engagement-show-employees-where-they-fit-in/524725/.

[139] Tony Schwartz and Christina Porath, "The Power of Meeting Your Employees' Needs," *Harvard Business Review*, June 30, 2014, https://hbr.org/2014/06/the-power-of-meeting-your-employees-needs.

[140] Victor Lipman, "66% Of Employees Would Quit if They Feel Unappreciated," *Forbes*, June 25, 2018, www.forbes.com/sites/victorlipman/2017/04/15/66-of-employees-would-quit-if-they-feel-unappreciated/.

[141] "Employees Want to Feel a Sense of Purpose at Work," Hays Recruiting, Novermer 2, 2016, https://www.hays.cn/en/press-releases/HAYS_1388244.

[142] "Why Retraining Is the New Recruiting," Workopolis, March 8, 2018, hiring.workopolis.com/article/retraining-new-recruiting/.

[143] Joseph Lawler and Alan Diaz, "More People Quit Their Jobs in December than Anytime in 16 Years," *Washington Examiner*, February 6, 2018, www.washingtonexaminer.com/more-people-quit-their-jobs-in-december-than-anytime-in-16-years.

[144] "The Great Training Budget Boom of 2017," *Panopto*, April 9, 2018, www.panopto.com/blog/the-great-training-budget-boom-of-2017/.

[145] Michael J. Coren, "Google's Latest Hiring Tactic Is Training Other Companies' Employees," *Quartz*, January 16, 2018, work.qz.com/1180907/google-will-pay-to-train-10000-it-specialists-it-may-never-hire/.

[146] Susan Caminiti, "AT&T's $1 Billion Gambit: Retraining Nearly Half Its Workforce for Jobs of the Future," CNBC, March 13, 2018, www.cnbc.com/2018/03/13/atts-1-billion-gambit-retraining-nearly-half-its-workforce.html.

[147] John Donovan and Cathy Benko, "Inside AT & T's Talent Overhaul," *Harvard Business Review*, October 2016, https://hbr.org/2016/10/atts-talent-overhaul.

Chapter 7

[148] Ed Frauenheim, "Contingent Workers: Why Companies Must Make Them Feel Valued," *Workforce*, August 3, 2012, http://www.workforce.com/2012/08/03/contingent-workers-why-companies-must-make-them-feel-valued.

[149] "Contingent Worker Job Experience in Context: Strength and Opportunity Areas," Willis Towers Watson, May 2018.

[150] Robert McGuire, "If Freelancers Are Key Partners, Are You Developing Them," *Venture Beat*, October 23, 2016, https://venturebeat.com/2016/10/23/if-freelancers-are-key-partners-are-you-developing-them/.

151 Daniel Coyle, *The Culture Code: The Secrets of Highly Successful Groups* (New York: Bantam Books, 2018), 23–24.

152 Alison Doyle, "What Is Telecommuting?" *The Balance*, June 11, 2018, https://www.thebalancecareers.com/what-is-telecommuting-2062113.

153 "20-Year Employee Benefits Trends in the United States—Then and Now," Society for Human Resource Management, June 20, 2016, https://www.shrm.org/about-shrm/press-room/press-releases/pages/2016-employee-benefits-survey-news-release.aspx.

154 Annamarie Mann and Amy Adkins, "America's Coming Workplace: Home Alone," Gallup, March 15, 2017, https://news.gallup.com/businessjournal/206033/america-coming-workplace-home-alone.aspx.

155 Statistics Canada, "Journey to Work: Key Results from the 2016 Census," *The Daily*, November 29, 2017, https://www150.statcan.gc.ca/n1/daily-quotidien/171129/dq171129c-eng.htm.

156 "Being Sick of Your Daily Commute Could Be Affecting Your Health," National Health Service (U.K.), August 24, 2016, https://www.nhs.uk/news/lifestyle-and-exercise/being-sick-of-the-daily-commute-could-be-affecting-your-health/.

157 Andrea Loubier, "Benefits of Telecommuting for the Future of Work," *Forbes*, July 20, 2017, https://www.forbes.com/sites/andrealoubier/2017/07/20/benefits-of-telecommuting-for-the-future-of-work/#339bfee616c6.

158 "Telecommuting Could Save U.S. Over $700 Billion a Year and Much More," *Global Workplace Analytics*, http://globalworkplaceanalytics.com/cut-oil.

159 Leanna Garfield and Jenny Cheng, "The Income Needed to Afford a Median-Priced Home in San Francisco Bay Area County," *Business Insider*, June 8, 2018, http://www.businessinsider.com/san-francisco-bay-area-what-it-costs-to-live-2018-6.

160 Royal LePage Real Estate Services, "From a Studio Apartment to a Large Detached Home: What the Average Peak Millennial Can Afford Across Canada," Cision, April 26, 2018, https://www.newswire.ca/news-releases/from-a-studio-apartment-to-a-large-detached-home-what-the-average-peak-millennial-can-afford-across-canada-680909031.html.

161 April McCullum, "Vermon Will Pay Remote Workers $10,000 to Move Here," *Burlington Free Press*, May 31, 2018, https://www.burlingtonfreepress.com/story/news/local/vermont/2018/05/31/vermont-pay-remote-workers-move-incentive/659553002/.

[162] Murad Hemmadi, "70% of Millennial Workers Would Rather Tele-commute than Come to the Office," *Canadian Business*, June 24, 2014, https://www.canadianbusiness.com/business-strategy/millennials-pre-fer-telecommuting/.

[163] Shana Lynch, "Why Working from Home Is a 'Future-looking Technol-ogy,'" *Stanford Business*, June 22, 2017, https://www.gsb.stanford.edu/insights/why-working-home-future-looking-technology.

[164] Kara Swisher, "'Physically Together': Here's the Internal Yahoo No-Work-from-Home Memo for Remote Workers and Maybe More," *All Things D*, February 3, 2013, http://allthingsd.com/20130222/physically-together-heres-the-internal-yahoo-no-work-from-home-memo-which-extends-be-yond-remote-workers/.

[165] Omar El Akkad, "Richard Branson Blasts Mayer's Telework Stand at Ya-hoo," *Globe and Mail*, May 11, 2018, https://www.theglobeandmail.com/report-on-business/careers/the-future-of-work/richard-branson-blasts-mayers-telework-stand-at-yahoo/article9296083/.

[166] Jane Gomez, "Remote Working: Three Sticking Points Managers Need to Get Over," Virgin, May 7, 2015, https://www.virgin.com/disruptors/remote-working-three-sticking-points-managers-need-get-over.

[167] Alex "Sandy" Pentland, "The Water Cooler Effect," *Psychology Today*, November 22, 2009, https://www.psychologytoday.com/intl/blog/reali-ty-mining/200911/the-water-cooler-effect.

[168] Kyodo, "Japan's Telecommuters Work to Clear Communication Hurdles amid Government Push," *Japan Times*, February 14, 2018, https://www.japantimes.co.jp/news/2018/02/14/national/social-issues/japans-tele-commuters-work-clear-communication-hurdles-amid-government-push/#.W0OUw9hKjow.

[169] Shashank Nigam, "How We Re-Designed Work Culture at SimpliFlying in the Last Six Years (and Our Bold New Experiment)," SimpliFlying, April 15, 2016, http://simpliflying.com/2016/how-we-re-designed-work-culture-at-simpliflying-in-the-last-six-years-and-our-bold-new-experiment/.

[170] Sonny Chheng, Kelly Monahan, Karen Reid, "Beyond Office Walls and Balance Sheets: Culture and the Alternative Workforce," *Deloitte Review* 21 (July 31, 2017), https://www2.deloitte.com/insights/us/en/deloitte-re-view/issue-21/workplace-culture-and-alternative-workforce.html.

[171] Shashank Nigam, "The SimpliFlying Compulsory Leave Experiment—the Results Are In!" LinkedIn, November 21, 2016, https://www.linke-din.com/pulse/simpliflying-compulsary-leave-experiment-results-sha-shank-nigam-/?published=t.

[172] Adam Putz and Anthony Mirhaydari, "Why Netflix Isn't the Key to Apple's Streaming Dream," PitchBook, July 9, 2018, https://pitchbook.com/news/articles/why-netflix-isnt-the-key-to-apples-streaming-dream.

173 Daniel Newman, "Coexisting with Robots—the Future Workplace Reality," *Future of Work*, September 18, 2017, https://fowmedia.com/coexisting-with-robots-the-future-workplace-reality/.

174 Lynda Gratton and Andrew Scott, "People Are Living Longer and Working Longer—but Few Organizations Have Come to Terms with the Opportunities and Challenges that Greater Longevity Brings," *MIT Sloan Management Review*, Spring 2017, https://sloanreview.mit.edu/article/the-corporate-implications-of-longer-lives/.

Chapter 8

175 "World Economic Outlook, October 2017: Seeking Sustainable Growth," International Monetary Fund, October 2017, https://www.imf.org/en/Publications/WEO/Issues/2017/09/19/world-economic-outlook-october-2017.

176 Annie Lowrey, *Give People Money: How a Universal Basic Income Would End Poverty, Revolutionize Work, and Remake the World* (New York: Crown, 2018).

177 Joi Ito, "The Paradox of Universal Basic Income," *Wired*, March 29, 2018, https://www.wired.com/story/the-paradox-of-universal-basic-income/

178 For more, see Wayne Simpson, Greg Mason, and Ryan Godwin, "The Manitoba Basic Annual Income Experiment: Lessons Learned 40 Years Later, *Canadian Public Policy* 43, no. 1 (March 2017) 85–104, https://umanitoba.ca/media/Simpson_Mason_Godwin_2017.pdf.

179 Harriet Agerholm, "Universal Basic Income: Half of Britons Back Plan to Pay All UK Citizens Regardless of Employment," *Independent*, September 11, 2017, https://www.independent.co.uk/news/uk/home-news/universal-basic-income-benefits-unemployment-a7939551.html.

180 Chris Deaton, "It's Low Unemployment for Everyone," *Weekly Standard*, July 7, 2018, https://www.weeklystandard.com/chris-deaton/the-unemployment-rate-for-high-school-graduates-and-college-graduates-is-converging.

181 David Hodges, "Rapid Growth of Automation Threatening Jobs in Canada: Report," Global News, October 19, 2017, https://globalnews.ca/news/3812887/canadian-jobs-automation-technology/.

182 Natasha Lomas, "UI Outs Plan to Bolster Gig Economy Workers Rights," Tech Crunch, February 7, 2018, https://techcrunch.com/2018/02/07/uk-outs-plan-to-bolster-gig-economy-workers-rights/.

183 Yuki Noguchi, "Gig Economy Renews Debate Over Whether Contractors Are Really Employees," NPR, March 7, 2018, https://www.npr.org/2018/03/07/589840595/gig-economy-renews-debate-over-whether-contractors-are-really-workers.

[184] Maurie Beckman, "Gig Workers Aren't Saving for Retirement. Here's How They Can Do Better," The Motley Fool, June 11, 2018, https://www.fool.com/retirement/2018/06/11/gig-workers-arent-saving-for-retirement-heres-how.aspx.

[185] TD Bank, "Pervasive and Profound: The Impact of Income Volatility on Canadians," https://td-capa.s3.amazonaws.com/prod/default/0001/02/a5a362538f70b81df4ae6ea6d66e8171cbd444ca.pdf.

[186] Annie Nova, "16 Percent of Workers Can't Get Unemployment Insurance. How to Fix That," CNBC, February 22, 2018, https://www.cnbc.com/2018/02/22/how-to-help-the-16-percent-of-workers-without-unemployment-insurance.html.

[187] Government of Canada, "Update of Long-Term Economic and Fiscal Projections 2017," Department of Finance, December 22, 2017, https://www.fin.gc.ca/pub/ltefp-peblt/2017/report-rapport-eng.asp.

[188] Taylor Jackson and Jason Clemens, "Canada's Aging Population is Going to Put a Strain on Government Coffers," Maclean's, October 31, 2017, https://www.macleans.ca/opinion/canadas-aging-population-is-going-to-put-a-strain-on-government-coffers/.

[189] Lydia O'Neal, "Who Ends Up Paying for the Gig Economy?" International Business Times, May 3, 2017, https://www.ibtimes.com/political-capital/who-ends-paying-gig-economy-uber-airbnb-make-millions-while-states-lose-out.

[190] Theodore Bunker, "Bridgewater Founder: Universal Basic Income Would Cost Nearly $4T," Newsmax, July 12, 2018, https://www.newsmax.com/us/dalio-ubi-trillions/2018/07/12/id/871387/.

[191] Dylan Matthews, "Hillary Clinton Almost Ran for President on a Universal Basic Income," Vox, September 12, 2017, https://www.vox.com/policy-and-politics/2017/9/12/16296532/hillary-clinton-universal-basic-income-alaska-for-america-peter-barnes.

[192] Chris Weller, "Bill Gates Says Robots That Tax Your Job Should Pay Taxes," Business Insider, February 17, 2017, https://www.businessinsider.com/bill-gates-robots-pay-taxes-2017-2.

Postscript

[193] Corinne Purtill, "A Stanford Researcher Says We Should Start Working Full Time until Age 40," Quartz at Work, June 27, 2018, https://qz.com/work/1314988/stanford-psychologist-laura-carstensen-says-careers-should-be-mapped-for-longer-lifespans/.

INDEX

Graetz, George, 83
Grubhub, 186-187

Haldane, Andy, 73
Hansen, Michael E., 117
Hanson, Gordon H., 51
happiness, and work, 16-17, 96-97,
    141-142
Harvard Business Review, 99, 141,
    147, 149, 168
Hays, 143
health. *See* stress.
health-care costs, 191-192
health-care occupations, 46, 79,
    116-117, 118
Hébert, Richard, 39
hiring practices, 28-38
Hollywood Model, 15, 148, 149,
    152-153
human resources departments (HR),
    131-133, 134, 151
Human Resources Professionals
    Association, 184-185
Huws, Ursula, 104

IBM, 157-158, 162
identity, and work, 10-11
immigration, 43, 47-51
income inequality, 58, 106-107, 111,
    123
income support programs, 172-
    173. *See also* universal basic
    income.
income taxes, 192. *See also* nega-
    tive income tax.
income volatility, 122-123, 125,
    172, 176-177, 178, 189
India, 32-33
industrial model, 23, 25-27, 193

Industrial Revolutions, 25, 64-84,
    197
inflation, 27
information technology jobs, 99-
    100
Institute for Global Prosperity
    (IGP), 181
Institute on Taxation and Economic
    Policy, 193
interactions, with co-workers, 164-
    167
interest rates, 52
International Monetary Fund (IMF),
    57, 173
Ipsos Research, 122-123

Japan, 52-53, 78, 81, 165
Jenkins, Antony, 81
job security, 18, 172. *See also* in-
    come volatility.
*Journal of Social Science and Medi-
    cine*, 112-113

Katz, Lawrence, 27-28, 97
Kelowna, B.C., 127-128
Keynes, John Maynard, 65-66
KFC, 33. *See also* PFK.
Kronos, 168-169
Krueger, Alan, 27-28, 97

labor-force participation, 27, 41-47,
    69-70. *See also* immigration.
labor income shares, 57
labor market, changes in, 16, 77,
    88-89, 114-119
labor supply, 36-37, 43-45
Laski, Amy, 165-166
law profession, 80

learning and development (L&D), 145
legislation, 171-195
LinkedIn, 140, 155
Liu, Chen, 51
local firms, 32-33
loneliness, 11, 126-127, 161
Luddites, 63, 64-65

Malcolm, Tracey, 154-155
Manta Group, 126
manufacturing sector, 36, 57-58, 70, 79, 83, 118
Marketplace, 113
Massachusetts Institute of Technology, 70-71, 79, 164-165
maternity benefits, 171-172, 189-190
Mayer, Marissa, 162
MBO Partners, 122
McAfee, Andrew, 70-71
McDonald's, 55, 76, 184
McIntosh, Craig, 51
McKinsey & Company, 91, 92-93, 96-97, 113, 116, 118, 134
McKinsey Global Institute, 74, 77
medical field. *See* health-care occupations.
Mexico, 50-51
Michaels, Guy, 83
Midwest Economic Policy Institute, 116
Millennial Generation, 40-41, 43, 44, 101, 103, 104-106, 160, 161
Mills, Terence, 26
Mincome, 180
minimum wage, 39, 65, 75, 77, 97, 121, 186-187

Montreal Gazette, 56
mothers, in the workforce, 11
multinationals, 32, 33
Myracing.com, 95

NAIRU (non-accelerating inflationary rate of unemployment), 47
NASA, 141, 143
Nation1099.com, 92
negative income tax, 177, 178-179
Neolithic Revolutions, 24
Netflix, 168, 170, 174
New York University, 185Nigam, Shashank, 166, 169
nursing workforce, 46

Oakley, Diane, 104
Office Angels, 162-163
office design, 139-141
oil, price of, 30-31
Old Age Security, 191
oligopoly, 35
onboarding, 154
online platforms, 90, 104, 121, 186-187
online retail, 84. *See also* Etsy; Teachers Pay Teachers.
open plan offices, 139-141
Organisation for Economic Co-operation and Development (OECD), 78-79, 124
Organization of the Petroleum Exporting Countries (OPEC), 31
OriHime, 165
Osborne, Michael, 78

parental leave, 171